D1084015

ONLY SON

ONLY SON

by WALTER FARRELL O. P.

SHEED AND WARD · NEW YORK · 1953

Library of Congress Catalog Number 53–12118

Third Printing, March 1954

Revisores Ordinis:
E. S. Carlson, O.P., S.T.M.
R. G. Joubert, O.P., PH.D., S.T.BACC.,
(*Ord. Praed.*)

Imprimi potest:
E. L. Hughes, O.P., S.T.LR.,
Prior Provincialis

Nihil obstat:
J. S. Considine, O.P., S.T.M.

Imprimatur:
✠ Samuel Cardinalis Stritch,
Archiepiscopus Chicagiensis

Die 15 Augusti, 1953.

MANUFACTURED IN THE UNITED STATES OF AMERICA

PUBLISHERS' NOTE

FOR TWO years Father Walter Farrell had been working on this life of Our Lord. Nine chapters were finished, and most of the tenth. He had come to the end of the page he was typing. Something interrupted him. Before he had an opportunity to sit down to his typewriter again, he was dead.

It was obvious that what he had written must be published. But its incompleteness posed a problem. The manuscript ended in mid-sentence, indeed in mid-text. The first idea was to ask some other writer to finish it; but Father Farrell's way of writing was entirely his own, anyone else's could only clash with it. Then it was remembered that in the Fourth Volume of his monumental *Companion to the Summa,* there were chapters on Our Lord's Death and Resurrection. This was the solution: these two chapters should be used: Father Farrell should complete Father Farrell, leaving no clash of styles to jar the reader's ear.

It only remained to fill the gap between Our Lord's discourse in Galilee, in the midst of which the manuscript ended, and His death on Calvary. This has been done by means of a summary, factual and without comment. That apart, everything in the book is Father Farrell's.

CONTENTS

ONLY SON

❖ I

THE INCARNATION

"IN THE sixth month, the angel Gabriel was sent from God into a city of Galilee, called Nazareth, to a virgin espoused to a man whose name was Joseph, of the house of David, and the Virgin's name was Mary" (Luke 1:26–27).*

The contrasting setting of the jewel was perfect. Nazareth had nothing of the fullness that makes up the pulsing life of a town. For all its location in Galilee, the most flourishing of King Herod's provinces, its only excuse for existence was its well. For all its pretentious name, "guardian" or "fortress," it was an utterly insignificant hamlet unmentioned anywhere but in the Gospels, though it held a commanding and beautiful view of the smooth stretch of the Plain of Esdrelon. From the archaeological findings, it had once had a fair number of inhabitants; but at the time of the angel's mission, its few dwellings were of the meanest: many of them no more than caves made habitable, others made up of a couple of rooms, one well sunk beneath

* Father Farrell follows the Douay-Rheims version of the Scriptures except in a few instances: e.g., Luke 3:13–15 (p. 76), where his own manuscript translation has been replaced by the Confraternity Edition (St. Anthony Guild Press).

the street level and hardly escaping from the classification of a cave. The hamlet was obscure, off the beaten track, poverty-stricken, and held in contemptuous disregard by the contemporaries of Our Lady.

It was into one of these lowly homes that the archangel came to find the Virgin whose name was Mary. The contrast would be striking, even to an angelic being, who is not forced to see the sharp beauty of truth in terms of contrast as is the way of our stumbling minds: here was the rich fullness which is the aim of men's longest dreams and God's great generosity. The virgin would present that lovely combination of a child's eyes and young womanhood's grace; she was about fourteen years old, with the early maturity of the East and the complete physical perfection assured by divine wisdom's preparation of the mother of God's Son. In her veins flowed the royal blood of the line of David, a title to deep respect from her compatriots for all her biting poverty. All this, however, was as nothing compared to the flood of divine life in her soul.

In preparation for this moment, she had been singularly preserved from the stain of original sin which, in all other children of Adam, made the beginnings of physical life simultaneous with spiritual death. Mary had never for an instant breathed the tainted air of sin. But this negative statement of the fact hides rather than reveals the full glory of the truth; its positive statement blinds the eyes. Because she was possessed of the divine life of grace from the first instant of her life, with nothing of unruly passions to retard her rush to the arms of God, Mary's every act was perfectly proportioned to the grace of that moment and thereby merited an increase in the vigor of divine life in her soul. Moment by moment, day by day, there was, then, a geometric increase in the divine life and divine love in her soul; until, at this moment of the angel's visit, the intensity and clarity of love in her heart would be beyond all computation.

Such goodness cannot be hidden by the veil of flesh; the rays of its glory would shine forth through the crevices of words, of actions, of eyes, of hands, of posture. The very common name of Mary, with its flattering connotation of Lady or Princess, was particularly proper to this virgin of Nazareth. She was indeed the gracious Lady, gracious in the fullest, most extensive sense of that word; so full of grace that Gabriel could dispense with her name and identify her by that very fullness which yet, by the merciful generosity of God, increased her capacity and constantly made room for yet more fullness.

"And the angel being come in, said unto her: Hail full of grace, the Lord is with thee. And she was troubled at his saying and thought within herself what manner of salutation this should be. And the angel said to her: Fear not, Mary, for thou hast found grace with God. Behold thou shalt conceive in thy womb, and shalt bring forth a son; and thou shalt call His name Jesus. He shall be great, and shall be called the Son of the Most High; and the Lord God shall give unto Him the throne of David His father; and He shall reign in the house of Jacob forever, and of His Kingdom there shall be no end. And Mary said to the angel: How shall this be done, because I know not man? And the angel answering, said to her: The Holy Ghost shall come upon thee, and the power of the Most High shall overshadow thee; and therefore the Holy which shall be born of thee shall be called the Son of God. And behold thy cousin Elizabeth, she also hath conceived a son in her old age;

and this is the sixth month with her that is called barren, because no word shall be impossible with God. And Mary said: Behold the handmaid of the Lord; be it done to me according to thy word. And the angel departed from her" (Luke 1:28–38).

Lest we miss any detail of this turning point in the history of the world, the divinely arranged contrasts continue. In the early fall, six months previously, the same archangel had appeared in the magnificence of the Temple at Jerusalem; here it was in the obscure poverty of a humble home. There he had found Zachary alone, but wrapped about with the priestly dignity and in the ennobling exercise of his priestly function; here Mary too was alone, but with all her dignity and nobility from within, stemming from the consuming fire of love of God. There, Zachary was so terrified by the vision that an immediate angelic reassurance was necessary to restore the use of his faculties; here there was the obeisance of the angel to his Queen and Mary's alert pondering of the angelic words. Zachary doubted the angel's word and demanded a sign; Mary's very question as to the *manner* of the conception was itself an immediate acceptance of the fact the angel announced. She asked for nothing and was given a sign that would be an invitation to her thoughtfulness, in contrast to Zachary's punitive sign that held him dumb before all the people. To Zachary was announced a conception to be achieved in the natural manner, to Mary, a conception that was openly and frankly above all nature's powers. Zachary rose up to return to his home and father the precursor, humbled, stricken by divine power, grateful even for the physical barrier against speech with his heart so full; with Mary, the divine wonder was accomplished when the humble words fell from her lips:

"Behold the handmaid of the Lord; be it done to me according to thy word."

The angel's mission was a great one, worthy of his sublime nature; yet it was a limited one. He was to win the instant and complete attention of the virgin, propose that she, by the power of God, become the mother of the Messias, and receive her consent. This he did within a perfection of economy which allowed St. Luke to record the memory of it, so sharply etched in the heart of the virgin, within the length of a paragraph. His salutation, "Hail full of grace" would startle a humble mind into immediate and complete attention; for the humbly wise see well the abyss that yawns between the most perfect of creatures and the absolute perfection which is God. It would be clear to the humblest maiden of Israel that it was the birth of the Messias which was in question from the angel's description of a son of David who was to be called Saviour, the Son of the Most High. The vistas of the supernatural were thrown open by the angel's flat statement of the miraculous nature of the conception and by the eternity promised to the kingdom of the Messias. The confirmatory evidence of Elizabeth's motherhood was sheer divine largesse. But it was not Gabriel's work to give an instruction on, or even to make a statement of, the mystery of the Incarnation. It was not because the child was to be miraculously conceived by divine power that He would be the Son of God, but because it was to be the eternally generated Son of God who was to take human nature from Mary; this divine Person, God from eternity by His divine nature, man in time by the human nature He was now assuming, this same Person was Son of God and was to be son of Mary. What instruction of this mystery was given to Mary would be the direct work of the Holy

Ghost; we cannot doubt its fullness, but we can never know from the lips of Mary the extent of the knowledge given her. She was always par excellence the keeper of the King's secret. Those who would learn of this mystery would learn it from God, not from her; for this was God's to tell.

Gabriel spoke in the name of divine wisdom; and he was answered with a wisdom that could only be from God. Mary was troubled at the extraordinariness of the salutation of the angel, pondering it within herself. Obviously, this was but a prelude to even more extraordinary things. It never occurred to Mary to doubt the truth of the angel's message; indeed, it was the common opinion of the time that the Messias would be born of the line of David, and the children of David had fallen on meagre times. There was no element of surprise in the prospect of the birth of the Messias in the humblest of circumstances rather than in the palace of the alien king. The surprising factor was that the proposal of the angel seemed to demand the surrender of the virginity which Mary had vowed to God; how could this conception of the Messias come about in the face of that vow? To the angelic intelligence, the difficulty was abundantly clear: this was not a question springing from naive ignorance, there was no forgetfulness on the part of Mary of her espousal to Joseph; the natural channels to conception were apparently quite clear. The question made sense only because with Joseph the virgin had embraced a perpetual virginity; and in this sense the difficulty was promptly met with an equal clarity of response from the angel. The eternal Son of God would have no temporal father; the power of God would come upon the virgin.

To some who blithely swallow the contradiction of

nothingness girding itself to become an ordered world, the virginal conception of Jesus Christ is beyond swallowing; but that the Father of all should dispense with one of his creatures and accomplish directly what his shared power has made possible to men, represented no difficulty to the virgin's wisdom. Given the disfavor in which virginity was held by the Jews, Mary's espousal to Joseph might be reason for doubt of the virginal vows of Mary and Joseph; but to those to whom the heights of virtue are not shocking impossibilities, and who can read the clear, calm words of the Gospel story it is not hard to believe that human love too can reach divine heights of generosity.

Mary's words of acceptance write the perfect conclusion to this most stupendous scene in human history: "Behold the handmaid of the Lord; be it done to me according to thy word." The most exact word is "slave," not "handmaid"; in other words, Mary has said behold one who is totally delivered up to God, wholly, completely His, one to whom the fulfillment of His desires will be all joy. It pleased the almighty God to stake the salvation of man on the response of the virgin of Nazareth; even for such priceless results, divinity will not force the will of man. The fate of mankind depended on the generous answer of this girl. When that answer was given, the Son of God was made man; this was the first instant of the life of Christ.

When the angel had departed from her, "Mary rising up in those days went into the hill country with haste into a city of Juda." This was not by any means the hectic hurry of flight inspired by worry, fright, or loneliness. Her haste was to an assured welcome where thoughtfulness would have the opportunities in which it delights, and the heart be free to say the secret things that are almost too much for it to contain. There would be preparations to be made. This, after all, was a journey of some four days for a visit that would last three months. With preparations complete, Our Lady would have to accommodate her departure to make connections with a troop of travellers to the south, for this was no journey to be taken alone; and thus, without loss of time, she set out for Ain-Karem, the home of her cousin Elizabeth, some four miles southwest of Jerusalem.

This was the first journey of Jesus Christ, God's Son made man. The hurried diligence and directness of the trip set the pattern for millions of other such journeys down through the ages, journeys whose goal of bringing the Son of God to men was the same, though it would be sacramental veils rather than the veil of humanity which hid the divine Person, and the pyx would be a tiny golden vessel hidden in the pocket of a priest rather than the womb of the Virgin Mother of God. From the exultant song that burst from Mary's heart as soon as it was at home with Elizabeth, we have an insight into the long thoughts and the mounting fires of love that crowded the hours of the journey with such precious silence, a silence familiar and dear to every Catholic who has received Holy Communion.

To appreciate the words of the two women on Mary's arrival at Elizabeth's home, several things must be kept well in mind. It must be remembered, for example, that Mary's visit was unannounced; her appearance on the threshold of her cousin was a complete surprise. The angel had told Mary no more than the fact of her miraculous conception of the Messias, while Elizabeth had been told nothing at all. We must remember, too, that Elizabeth was absorbed in the joy of a pregnancy long despaired of; and with the details of Zachary's wonderful tale of the angelic apparition to spur on a mother's natural speculation on the future of her child. In view of all this, the gospel account of that meeting of the two women is surprising in almost every detail. "When Elizabeth heard the salutation of Mary, the infant leaped in her womb. And Elizabeth was filled with the Holy Ghost: and she cried out with a loud voice, and said: 'Blessed art thou among women, and blessed is the fruit of thy womb. And whence is this to me, that the mother of my Lord should come to me? For behold as soon as the voice of thy salutation sounded in my ears, the infant in my womb leaped for joy. And blessed art thou that hast believed, because those things shall be accomplished that were spoken to thee by the Lord' " (Luke 1:41–45).

All Christendom has cherished the words of Elizabeth, uniting them to Gabriel's greeting to the Virgin in the beloved and unceasing prayer, the Ave Maria. That Elizabeth should have so completely forgotten herself and the divine favors done to her, that she should have offered instant obeisance to one so much her junior, that she should have been so fully informed of what was known only to Mary and to God, all this could have but the one explanation: Elizabeth was indeed filled with the Holy Ghost.

Elizabeth was the first to know that salvation had commenced, that the Messias had entered upon the scene; and her obviously complete knowledge released the joy pent up in Mary's heart from the moment of the Annunciation. She could speak now without betraying the King's secret; her answer to Elizabeth was worthy of her new dignity, the exultant *Magnificat*. No need to speak of Mary as being filled with the Holy Ghost;

she was the mother of the Lord, the Lord was with her, she was blessed above all women. Her joy broke forth in a torrent of praise and gratitude; here there was no question of talking of humility but of practising it. The acceptance of her cousin's congratulations is itself a contrast of the grandeur of divinity and the lowliness of any created perfection, the contrast that is the very heart of humility; in the white light of humility's truth, the mercy of God shines forth blindingly. Salvation has begun and will be continued according to the promises long since made by God.

"And Mary said: My soul doth magnify the Lord. And my spirit hath rejoiced in God my Saviour. Because He hath regarded the humility of His handmaid: for behold from henceforth all generations shall call me blessed. Because He that is mighty hath done great things to me: and holy is His name. And His mercy is from generation unto generations, to them that fear Him. He hath shewed might in His arm: He hath scattered the proud in the conceit of their heart. He hath put down the mighty from their seat and hath exalted the humble. He hath filled the hungry with good things: and the rich He hath sent empty away. He hath received Israel His servant, being mindful of His mercy. As He spoke to our fathers: to Abraham and to his seed for ever" (Luke 1:46–55).

It is true that the song of Mary was in complete accord with the custom of her time and her people; it is not surprising that, as any other woman of her time would, she draws upon the sacred writings of her people, specifically on the canticle of Anna and on the psalms. It presents no evidence of research or studied effort, it contains no original images, gives no evidence of personal poetic genius, none of the crashing figures that reverberate in the Book of Job; its material is all from the common sources of the chosen people. What lifts it above all other such songs is the sublime content of its rejoicing, the savoring perfection of the long thoughts of the Mother of God, and the one prophetic utterance confirming what so far exceeds the minds of men. Indeed all generations have called her blessed.

Mary stayed about three months with Elizabeth, that is until just before the birth of John the Baptist. She took her departure at the time when, because Elizabeth's secret would be made plain to the world, there would be plenty of neighborly help for her elderly cousin. The little town of Ain-Karem would soon rock with the joyful surprise of the birth of the Baptist, the divine unloosening of the tongue of Zachary, and the prophecies of the Benedictus that poured forth from that tongue freed at last as the no longer incredulous father wrote firmly of the infant "John is his name." But the delicacy of her people decreed that a house of delivery was no place for a virgin; then, too, Mary had no wish to incite curious questions from strangers as to her own condition, and there was Joseph, her espoused husband, waiting in far-off Nazareth in complete ignorance of the wonders God had worked in her. That just man must have been in the front of Mary's mind as she made her way north, for his faith would play no small part in the mystery of redemption, his faith in God and his faith in her.

It will be remembered that no word of the wondrous conception of the Saviour had been spoken aloud in Nazareth. All through Our Lady's life she played the part of the nourishing Mother of the Son of God, not His precursor; she spoke of God's secrets only after the mystery had first been revealed by God Himself. She had left Nazareth as quickly as possible after Gabriel's message some three months ago; she was returning now to parents and to Joseph who were still in the same complete ignorance in which she had left them. It must be remembered, too, that Mary was espoused to Joseph; or rather, she had been "given in marriage." For the Jewish espousals were quite different from what we understand by that word. Among Mary's people, the "giving in marriage" meant that the virgin passed from the power of her father to that of her husband, that she now had a new lord who could rightfully call her his wife. If her espoused husband were to die, she would be considered a widow; to break off the espousals required a bill of divorce. The espousal, in other words, was a true marriage; it was considered legally incomplete until there was an external passing from the father's to the husband's power, but the espousals themselves conferred full marriage rights.

The touching story of the events following on Our Lady's return to Nazareth is told succinctly in the first chapter of St. Matthew's gospel. Matthew's purpose was to bring out clearly the legal paternity of Joseph, so his whole story is told from the side of Joseph. With this stated in the genealogy, Matthew goes on to treat of the manner of this paternity; and here his chief interest is the miraculous manner of the conception of this legal son of Joseph who was by nature son of God and by nature son of Mary. There is, in fact, no mention of any other circumstance such as place and time. Matthew is writing from the fullness of revelation and the fullness of faith that was his; he is not leading his readers step by step, maintaining suspense until the great climax is reached. The divine truth is stated plainly. The formula of the genealogy, "begot," is changed in the last line directly referring to Our Lord to "was born"—"and Jacob begot Joseph, the husband of Mary, of whom was born Jesus." A few verses on is the flat statement: "When as his mother Mary was espoused to Joseph, before they came together, she was found with child of the Holy Ghost." By way of a last precaution against the calumnies of the Jews that may have already started in Matthew's time, the story closes with an equally flat statement: "And he knew her not till she brought forth her first-born son": a statement which clearly establishes the virginal birth of Christ, and does not, to one familiar with Jewish grammar and Jewish custom, mean that Our Lady had other children afterwards.

Short of a statement by Mary or a revelation by God, no one in Nazareth could know that Mary had conceived by the power of the Holy Ghost; neither of these was forthcoming. But it could not long be hidden that Our Lady had conceived. It would, in fact, be discovered almost immediately; not by Joseph, with whom she was not yet living, but most probably by her mother. In all fairness, Joseph would have to be told. To us, the astonishing thing is that he was not told by Mary, nor, after he had been informed, was there any word of explanation given him by his espoused wife. It is fortunate for us that Matthew tells the story. He, too, was a silent man—neither his own gospel nor the other three give us any word of his; he, too, had been snatched by divine invitation into the intimacy of things divine. That double bond of union gives his words a penetration which opens the heart of the silent Joseph, for an unending inspiration to the lowly and an unending humiliation of the mighty among those who dare to come close to God.

Mary's silence before Joseph and his dilemma in the

face of Mary's condition present the same difficulty to our minds and demand the same prerequisites for our understanding of them. Joseph's problem was not that of a wronged husband torn between justified anger and loving sympathy. It was much more serious than that. He was faced with a completely sure knowledge of two facts which were in open and evident conflict; he was as sure of the innocence and purity of Mary as he was of her pregnancy. He made no attempt to question either the one or the other. To grasp the dilemma of Joseph is at the same time to understand something of the stupendous confidence of Mary in her young husband's faith (Joseph was only twenty-three or twenty-four) though no word of hers had given him a shred of support for that faith. These things are not to be explained on human grounds. We fly in the face of the evidence if we picture Joseph as an easy-going, indulgent or spineless husband; Mary a naively ignorant, starry-eyed romantic. Even the sublime heights of human love's instant and unstinting generosity will not explain Joseph's sure knowledge or Mary's silent trust. For an insight into these things, we must recall Mary's sinless perfection and Joseph's worthiness to be her husband and the foster-father of God; we must see something of the fullness of grace that had been poured into their souls, the giant growth of the virtues from that divine life, and the intuitively divine action of the gifts of the Holy Ghost within them. Mary's heart could and did share something of the confidence of God through the gift of Fortitude; Joseph's mind could and did share something of the knowledge of God through the gift of Knowledge. In both cases, the results would be sure beyond all wavering, complete beyond all analysis, instant beyond all reasoning or argument; for by these gifts a man acts in the divine mode. Joseph did know the innocence and purity of Mary as surely, and as mysteriously, as one who is pure through the grace of God detects impurity long before its evidence can be presented to the rational processes.

Joseph is rightly described as just; the minimum meaning of that justice would be to give God and neighbor what is their due. Because of this justice, he was unwilling publicly to denounce Our Lady; which is to say, that such a denouncement would be an injustice to Mary. Her innocence, in other words, forbade a criminal proceeding against her. The law gave an espoused husband the right to proceed against his espoused wife in the face of such evidence as was plainly to Joseph's hand, but nowhere did the law command such a procedure; custom covered the case by allowing the husband to cede his rights if he liked: a bill of divorce could be given quietly, with no mention of time, and the guilty party freed to contract marriage with the father of her child.

Immediate action was demanded on Joseph's part. Three courses were open to him: he could denounce Mary publicly, exposing her to capital punishment or at least to public infamy; he could repudiate her secretly, minimizing the scandal, perhaps avoiding it altogether by freeing her to marry another; or he could legally complete the marriage, taking Mary into his house and assuming the legal paternity of her son. The first of these possibilities was firmly and completely rejected by Joseph; this would suppose Mary's guilt, a thing which Joseph's mind unwaveringly rejected. The second choice was the one dictated by human prudence in the name of loving mercy; yet it too demanded admission of a guilty act on Mary's part, even though every extenuating circumstance be conjectured to absolve her as far as possible from subjective fault. This line of action would, naturally and humanly, be considered by Joseph; yet against it stood the unshaken certainty of Mary's complete innocence. The third course of action was the one dictated by Our Lady's virtue, by the heart of Joseph, and, ultimately by the counsel of God through the mouth of an angel.

Of this last course, Joseph was definitely afraid. But what was there to fear? He was sure of Mary's innocence and of her love for him; the whole thing was secret, so there was no question of public opinion, no threat of scandal or mockery; there was nothing to fear for Mary safe in his house; as for himself, surely he would fear more than anything else to lose Mary. The fear of Joseph is clear only if we understand the nature of his dilemma, if we see that he was not in an agony of doubt of the fidelity of Mary; rather, he could not help suspecting that there was something beyond all understanding, which is to say, something divine. To mix oneself in divine things, to dare to advance by one's own decision into an intimacy with the living God, to push one's way into the sanctuary unbidden, these are things of which a man might well be afraid. Joseph's hesitation was not a doubt of Mary but a fear of almighty God.

"But while he thought on these things, behold the angel of the Lord appeared to him in his sleep, saying: Joseph, son of David, fear not to take unto thee Mary thy wife, for that which is conceived in her is of the Holy Ghost" (Matt. 1:20). Here was the divine justification of Mary's silence; "the divine approval of the justice of Joseph's silence." Here was the divine invitation to a responsibility of which Joseph had proved himself worthy. The angel went on: "she shall bring forth a son; and thou shalt call His name Jesus. For He shall save His people from their sins." As in the case of Gabriel's appearance to Our Lady, no more is told than the fact of the Messianic character of the child and its miraculous conception; the unfolding of the mystery is for later days, and by the Son of God Himself.

From the angel's words, it is clear that until now Joseph had had no word that Mary's pregnancy was by a miracle of God's power. The darkness has been a challenge to his faith; and the part he is given in the mystery is patently quiet, obscure. His faith is confirmed by a divine informant, but not until his legal paternity is necessary for Mary and the child. There is sharp contrast between the daylight appearance of Gabriel and the interchange between the virgin and the archangel, and the appearance in a dream that reduces Joseph's part to a minimum. Joseph has no part to play here, no answers to give, no questions to ask. He has only to obey, taking his part humbly in the shadows where he will remain; the strong defender and provider of the Holy Family, but quiet, obscure, humble, silent in an awed gratitude for the love of God's mother and the joy of the child.

"And Joseph rising up from sleep, did as the angel of the Lord had commanded him, and took unto him his wife. And he knew her not till she brought forth her first-born son: and he called His name Jesus." Joseph's obedience was prompt, immediate, as well it might be from the love in his heart and the heavenly confirmation of his knowledge of Mary's purity. Mary was now at home with her family. The visit to Elizabeth is evidence enough of Mary's willingness, even eagerness, to open her bursting heart when God had made it no longer necessary to keep the incredible secrets. The gospel story leaves us with a heart-free Mary at home in the house of her young husband, who had given such striking proof of the depths of his love; at home, with all the quiet months of pregnancy before her, and all the smooth days of that humble living in Nazareth. Each day Joseph would have ever more reason to be quiet.

2

THE BIRTH OF THE SAVIOUR

NORMALLY the days of the first year of marriage are days of peace and wonder as the marvels of love unfold themselves. The days move swiftly, yet not swiftly enough to restrain the mounting anticipation of the birth of the child. The private lives of the couple flow smoothly into the sea of common life and are lost in its strength and power. Love builds up its invincible towers; security is an invigorating tang in every breath the couple breathes, for all the responsibilities, the burdens, the hard new things that stretch out challengingly ahead. Such days will not be seen again until, with life behind them, the man and wife are again alone awaiting the beginning of another life, the eternal life with God.

Mary and Joseph had almost the full complement of these priceless, personal days together. It was not until some five or six months after Mary had come to Joseph's house that the edict of Caesar Augustus put an end to their home life and set their feet on the road. That imperial edict enrolling the whole world was a matter of shock and disappointment in a little home much too insignificant for imperial consideration. Mary would have made plans for the reception of the Son of God; though they would have to be drawn within the limits set by poverty, at least they would have the familiarity of homely things and the generous friendliness of townsfolk no richer than the Holy Family itself. It could not be easy to see those plans shrunk to the proportions of swaddling clothes, home exchanged for the high road, and the prospect of a vagabond birth for her child among strangers. Mary's difficulties, as everything of Mary, were also Joseph's, with the added burden of the intense responsibility so properly the agony of a young husband.

Inconvenient and disagreeable, the trip had to be made. The edict was plain, and clearly understood since it was so in harmony with the customs of the country. Everyone in the East, then as now, knows his clan or family group and the city of its origin; that spot is always home however far the feet may wander over the face of the earth. In a small country, like the Palestine of Joseph's time, this method of counting the people would not be impractical; and it would be entirely within the governing skill of the Romans to fit the search for sources of tax money into the framework of agreeable local custom. By the terms of the edict, Joseph would have to go to the city of David; i.e., to the place of David's birth, Bethlehem, not to the place of his glory or his burial, the kingly city of Jerusalem; for Joseph was of the family of David. The question as to whether it was necessary for Mary to go to Bethlehem has interested the scholars, the argument against it stemming from a denial of her Davidic ancestry; but St. Luke's insistence here that Joseph was of kingly origin is not a way of saying that Mary was not—St. Luke has already, in the story of the Annunciation, given strong indication of the origin of Mary from the same stock. At any rate, the question is academic; to a couple as much in love as Mary and Joseph, and at this supreme moment of expectation of the divine child, the question would much more likely be whether or not it could possibly be arranged that they could remain together.

As the memory of Our Lady recorded it years later for St. Luke, there was no debate about her accompanying her husband. In completely matter-of-fact terms the story is told much as we would have expected it: "Joseph also went up from Galilee, out of the city of Nazareth into Judea, to the city of David, which is called Bethlehem: because he was of the house and family of David, to be enrolled with Mary his espoused wife, who was with child" (Luke 2:4–5).

Obedience to the imperial command offered difficulties worthy of Joseph's broad shoulders. After all, he was a poor man; some of the Fathers think he was so poor as to be unable to afford that universal beast of burden, the diminutive ass that is still depended on for transportation of men and goods. Even if this were not within his own means, it would hardly seem likely that the journey would have to be made on foot by Our Lady. Human nature does not change: the ready helpfulness of the poor would not be less in Joseph's time, nor would the appeal of the beauty and goodness of Mary, the unselfish strength and neighborliness of Joseph, fail to win help to meet so obvious and so serious a difficulty. There was much more reason for uneasiness in the necessary interruption of Joseph's labors by a journey that must, in his most optimistic human calculations, consume close to two weeks. The poor have no reserves to call upon; their daily existence is a matter of delicate balance between calloused hand and hungry mouth. To arrest the working hand even for a day is a serious threat to the poor; and, as it turned out, the journey was to last not weeks but months. Even granting the easy hospitality of the East, some provision would have to be made for survival during the absence from Nazareth; quite aside from the lack of earnings, this would have been another of the serious problems faced by the husband of Mary.

Mary herself would be Joseph's greatest concern. It is true that idle curiosity, sentimental or vulgar speculations, detailed inquiries about the condition of Our Lady, are forever barred by the superb tact and delicate brevity of the words of St. Luke: "Mary, his espoused wife, who was with child." Still with the miraculous character of the child's conception well in mind, we must remember that all the rest of the long period of the nourishment of her child within herself proceeded along entirely natural lines. For all of St. Luke's careful stressing of the virginity of Mary, such as the craftsman's wise selection of the word "espoused," he does not attempt to gloss over the part left for nature to play in the coming of the Son of God; she was with child and her days were nearly fulfilled. It would be this that would loom large enough in Joseph's mind to overshadow, indeed to determine, every other consideration of his preparations for the journey to Bethlehem. Yet the privilege of worry would be cherished by Joseph, even without the superabundant compensation of his daily vision of the full bloom of beauty bestowed on Mary by her approaching motherhood.

The journey that stretched before the holy couple was of about eighty-five or ninety miles. It could be made without hurry by easy stages in about four days; and of course it would not be made in a solitary fashion that would expose the travellers to the dangers of the high road. Mary and Joseph could easily join one of the caravans following the main road south, joining such a group just a few miles from Nazareth itself. Because of the universal character of the imperial edict, travel would be much heavier than usual and this phase of the preparations for the trip would entail no difficulty.

So it was that one day in the late fall, Mary and Joseph left their village and their home and came down from the heights of Nazareth to the beautiful plain of Esdrelon, the garden of Israel and the warring place of the nations through the centuries. From there, they mounted slowly through the hill country to the mountainous territory of Judaea with its citadel and holy place of Jerusalem; on past the holy city some four or five miles to the city of David, the town of Bethlehem. The heat of the sun was pleasant at mid-day, the bite in the air sharp morning and evening, with a kind of bitterness in it during the placid hours of the night.

Joseph was of the family of David, directly descended from the great King; a circumstance which undoubtedly would, under ordinary conditions, have given him title to special consideration in the home of the clan. But these were no ordinary conditions. As they neared their destination, Joseph had more and more reason for uneasiness. There were crowds converging on the little town, and Joseph and Mary were by no means the first-comers. The town was full to overflowing. Even in the inn there was no room. Later on Joseph could easily agree that it was just as well. The inn, or khan, was designed much more for shelter against marauders than as protection against the sky; in its crowded condition, it certainly could not have offered more than a place for a man to bed down beside his animals and as close as possible to his fellows, with no more than safety for his comfort. An ill-fitting place indeed for the Virgin Mary to bring forth the Son of God. The last resort for the young protector of the Holy Family was one of the caves or grottoes in the hillside often used to shelter both men and animals.

That it was indeed one of these caves in which Mary and Joseph sought shelter is made clear by St. Luke's record of the manger used as a crib; for animals were not kept in the houses of that time. The use of the manger for the child was not at all unusual; in fact it was so ordinary among the poor that the portable manger used to feed the animals along the road was commonly used as a resting place for infants. Christian art has portrayed the cave of the nativity as actually having animals in it, the ox and the ass giving up their feeding place for the comfort of their God. The tradition is attested to by Origen and Jerome, proof enough that it did not have its source in the apocryphal gospels whose falsity Jerome hated so bitterly. The implications of the presence of animals in the cave are both plain and heartening. It would mean that the crowding of the town had long since filled even emergency shelters such as the caves; and Joseph, rather than merely chancing upon an empty cave, benefited by the eager thoughtfulness so common in even the roughest of men in the presence of impending motherhood. In any age, men would readily give up their shelter for one such as Mary awaiting her child. There is, however, nothing in the gospel story to justify a picture of a race between the discovery of a roof and the birth of the child; it might well have been several days after their arrival that Mary gave birth to her son. The point made so clearly by St. Luke, under the guiding memory of Mary, was that it was in the cave that the Son of God made His entry into the world of men.

The story of those moments so cherished by the world deserves the best of artistry in its telling. Our Lady, through the pen of St. Luke, gets it told with all the dramatic effectiveness of simplicity: "And it came to pass, that when they were there, her days were accomplished, that she should be delivered. And she brought forth her firstborn son, and wrapped Him up in swaddling clothes, and laid Him in a manger; because there was no room for them in the inn" (Luke 2:6–7). The quiet peace of the cave had a dim echo in the world outside of it, where no men were at war but few indeed at peace. The obscurity of Bethlehem was heightened in the dimness of the cave. The chill of winter penetrated to the depths of this rude shelter and found only Mary and Joseph; the darkness of the night was nature's guarantee of privacy for this sacred moment. Joseph was there, but he was more than ever in the shadows. This was Mary's moment, and she was completely adequate for it. The power of God had intervened to begin this life in the virginal womb; now, after the finish of the long months, that omnipotent power works again to effect a virgin birth, exultant, not sorrowful, untouched by pain, undamaging to virginal integrity. The same power that fended off the corruption of sin in the very beginnings of Mary's own life by the Immaculate Conception, preserved the virginity of Our Lady before birth and in birth, as it was later to forestall the corruption of death by the Assumption of the Virgin into heaven.

Mary's moment. And Joseph in the shadows would marvel at the instant expertness of this child-mother where his very strength would seem a threat to life's fragile beginning. The light of the world now shone in the cave and lighted up the face of the virgin mother in her adoring ministrations, to give Joseph a vision of beauty never to be granted another man in all the history of the world. To his humiliation there was the sharp consciousness of the crudeness of the cave, poverty's poor offering of swaddling-clothes, and the long prospect of nothing better than the most meagre days shaped by his hands; to his exultation, and a challenge to his strength, there was the helplessness of the divine infant, the youth of the Mother, and the serene trust of both in Joseph's providence. This infant, being God, had *chosen* all the details of his birth: the time, the place, Mary and Joseph. For all of his days it would be incredible to Joseph that the Mother of God and her child should have been entrusted to his care. The evasions of corrupt men in later ages were not possible to Joseph; for him there could be no doubt of the divine maternity. He was a witness, divinely instructed as to the person conceived by Mary, and the sole witness privileged to be present at the birth of that person; to be sure, only the human nature was taken from Mary, but it is the person who is born, not the nature—and here the person was the Second Person of the Blessed Trinity, the eternal Son of God. Joseph would remain in the shadows, and never cease wondering.

The heights of love reached by the hearts of Mary and her child in those first few moments will never be scaled by human words. To understand that, even in some small degree, we must see beyond the sweeping generosity of the sinless heart of this young mother, beyond the beauty of her face bent in adoration close above the face of the newborn infant. For alone, of all the infants born into the world, this one was aware of the warming love His mother wrapped around him. Though, like all infants, He was unable to focus His gaze, He knew the heart of Mary: knew it as God knows the heart of women, knew it as the blessed know the hearts of those dearest to them in the vision of God, knew it with that intuitive knowledge that is the birthright of the angels. From the first instant of life, the infant had known and had returned the love of His mother, and, returning it, fanned it to ever brighter, more intense flame. For Mary, these were not the precious moments for memory to retain unshared, a one-sided splendor which the infant could never know; these were shared moments, and every detail of her motherly goodness was savored with full appreciation by this divine child in her arms. It is no wonder that Luke joins Joseph in his silence, and turns his staggered mind from the invisible glory of the cave to the singing glory of the skies over the hillsides of Bethlehem.

"And there were in the same country shepherds watching, and keeping the night-watches over their flocks" (Luke 2:8). To this day, the shepherds keep this watch over their flocks just outside of Bethlehem; from the character of the soil, it has always been thus— an area of pasturage beyond the cultivated fields. Tradition places the field of the shepherds about a half-hour east of Bethlehem where the temperature is already considerably milder because the territory is so much lower than that of Bethlehem. The shepherds, then as now, were the desert shepherds, Bedouins who spent their lives in the open and to whom Bethlehem was much more a capital than Jerusalem. Sheep of the inhabitants of Bethlehem would long since have been gathered into shelters for the winter; these desert shepherds would have no more than a tent or a rude cabin from which to guard their flock throughout the night. These were rough, simple men, not searching old scrolls by torchlight, but working and re-working a few great truths in the lonely light of the stars to a harvest of great wisdom. They were Jews, and so to them angels would be familiar characters in the stories handed down from age to age; now, in their own lives, all those old stories would take on new life.

"And behold an angel of the Lord stood by them, and the brightness of God shone round about them; and they feared with a great fear" (Luke 2:9). Wrapped about with a brightness which St. Luke calls "of God," well they might fear with a great fear, even without the presence of an angel of the Lord. Yet, as was immediately evident, this was not an angel of vengeance. Instead of a flaming sword, he brought comfort against their fears and fulfillment of the hopes that had been the very lifeblood of this people for centuries upon centuries, cherished through countless starlit nights by just such simple men; joyous news indeed and for all the people, not merely for the shepherds. The momentous words would be etched indelibly in their memory and the memory of their children: "This day is born to you a Saviour, who is Christ the Lord, in the city of David. And this shall be a sign unto you. You shall find the infant wrapped in swaddling clothes, and laid in a manger" (Luke 2:11–12). There could be no mistaking the significance of the message; every word of it was impregnated with a Messianic flavor: the city of David, a Saviour, Christ the Lord, the only Lord, joyous tidings. It was the shepherds, not the angel, who were bathed in the brightness of God, for they it was who needed the light; lest that brightness and the momentous message overwhelm their minds or lead them to evade a truth too good to be true by resorting to an explanation that would dismiss the whole thing as an illusion, there was the touch of divine graciousness, even of divine humor adding a sign of prosaic human life to confirm the already startling sign written in the skies. A newborn infant, wrapped in swaddling-clothes; this was something a man could test for himself, here his feet would be on solid ground however high his head in the clouds. Then the sky split open "and suddenly there was with the angel a multitude of the heavenly army, praising God and saying: Glory to God in the highest; and on earth peace to men of good will" (Luke 2:13–14).

Perhaps the shepherds would miss the note of universality that extended these joyous tidings to all men of good will; they would not miss what was obvious to all their race, that men are not saved against their will, that peace is bought at a price. St. Luke made it abundantly plain, in all of this story of the coming of the Son of God among men, that men must do their part, bring those dispositions summed up as good will. Other men and women would hear the joyous tidings this same night, but not at all with the good will of the shepherds. When the last angelic note had died out of the night and the cloak of darkness was again slipped on the shoulders of the world, the shepherds set off in haste to Bethlehem, not dubiously or cynically, but in eager anticipation, to "see this word that is come to pass, which the Lord hath shewed to us." Just as the angel had said, they found Mary and Joseph, and the infant lying in a manger, "and seeing, they understood of the word that had been spoken to them concerning this child."

The shepherds would certainly explain their intrusion

into the family privacy of the cave, for simple men are seldom brazen. Their words would let Mary know that here again her heart was free to speak out the secrets of God, not betraying what He had already made known; no wonder that the shepherds understood. They in their turn would add one more divine item to the treasures beginning to be stored up in the heart of Our Lady: Gabriel's message, the revelation to Elizabeth, the merciful resolution of Joseph's fears, and now angelic multitudes singing in the sky to men who counted for so little in a world of Roman might. The events of the night were too much to be contained in the hearts of the shepherds; they talked, talked to all who would listen, and "all that heard, wondered; and at those things that were told them by the shepherds." They wondered; but Mary did more than wonder, she "kept all these words, pondering them in her heart." Wonder is too often no more than the splendor of a spark; and so it was here. The shepherds returned to their flocks glorifying and praising God; but the days took up their usual course and Jerusalem was undisturbed, the holy family as perfectly anonymous as if they were still hidden in the hills of Nazareth. His time had not yet come.

✣ 3

WISE MEN AND KINGS

AS THE shepherds disappeared into the night, glorifying the greatness of God and praising His works from the fullness of their faith, the privacy of obscurity swept into the cave, filling it with quiet and securing its entrance as solidly as a mountain barrier. The child and His mother, with Joseph, as the Evangelists so persistently and delicately phrase it in emphasis of Mary's virginity, now could move in and out and about their vagabond home with a freedom unsuspected by those caught in the spotlight of renown. Theirs was the usual lot of the poor and unknown; which means their hours were free for each other and for God.

The first week of the life of the Son of God on earth went by in this luxury of privacy. On the eighth day, the Law prescribed that a child be circumcised and given his name; on that day, Joseph, who loved the child with all the strength of his great heart, shed the first drops of the precious blood. On another day, men who hated him with all the strength of their envy and greed, would shed the last drop. Despite the difference in motive, these first drops, as well as the last, were of infinite worth for the salvation of men for they were the product of the suffering of an infinite Person. This fruit of

Joseph's religious obedience would in itself have been enough to satisfy for men if Christ had chosen it as His redemptive offering; but not enough to win their hearts. For that, an overwhelming manifestation of divinely reckless and generous love would hardly be enough. It is to be noted here that whatever the sorrow in the hearts of Joseph and Mary at this moment, it was only in the body of the child that there was pain suffered that men might live; here, as in the last moments of this divine life on earth, Mary's part was one of compassion. The pain and death belonged to her Son; it was He Who was the Saviour of men.

So the angels had called Him Saviour to the shepherds. This was the meaning of the name given beforehand to both Mary and Joseph by the angel. Here, in this ceremony of salvation, it was Joseph who conferred the holy name of Jesus on the child of Mary. There were no heavenly manifestations here, no prodigies, nothing to stun the human mind or heart, for the Son of God had not come to conquer men by His power but to save them by His sufferings and to win them by His love. This was a quiet, domestic affair entirely within the routine of any Jewish home; from the beginning and to the end of their life together, there were no manifestations of omnipotence in favor of the Son of Mary or of this holy family. This was merely one of the early steps in the path of humble obedience to the Law.

Though there was not, nor would ever be, sin in this child, there were reasons enough for Him to submit to circumcision which, as St. Thomas holds, was the sacrament of the Old Law in remedy of the original sin with which every child of the seed of Adam is born. It would be hard, though men would do it, to deny the reality of this body from which blood flowed and into which pain thrust its jagged edges. Here was divine approval of the divinely instituted sacrament of the Old Law. His own people would have less and less excuse for rejecting Him in the light of the full meaning of this eighth day of His life: here was a son of Abraham with the sign of salvation on him, a Jew respectful of and obedient to the Law, taking on Himself the full burden of the Law that men might ultimately be freed from it.

Forty days after the birth of the child, Mary with Jesus in her arms set off with Joseph on the journey to nearby Jerusalem. The few miles shrank under the sun of Mary's exultant joy in the clasp of the child, and were easily brushed behind her by steps made eager by a mother's happy sharing of the wonders of her child; for once a mother would be right, the world would indeed revolve around her child. Since the Law prescribed the ceremony of purification for the young mother forty days after the birth of a male child, Mary, like any Jewish mother of her time, would want to take advantage of the happy circumstance that found her so near to the Temple and so far from her home. So the days at Bethlehem were stretched out beyond the demands of the Roman census in order that the ceremony might take place in the very Temple itself. Mary had no need of the Law's protections against and remedies for sin; but the same divine reasons that submitted her Son to the Law demanded that she too bow to the Law's commands: humility, obedience, approval of the divine Law, a forestalling of the reasons that might be adduced by the Jews for rejecting herself and her Son.

The Law did not demand the presence of the child at this ceremony; its interest was the purification of the mother, who in this case needed no purification. St. Luke, telling the story years afterwards, is concerned with focusing attention on the presence of the child and His recognition as the Messias; indeed, humanly speaking, it would be hard to understand Mary needlessly leaving the child behind her, or Joseph allowing Mary to travel to Jerusalem and back without him. The young carpenter, his wife, and her child were in no position to offer the lamb and turtle dove in expiation for sin and in consecration of the child as demanded by the Law; they would have to take advantage of the provision in favor of the poor of substituting two pigeons. Besides this, there was the special ransom to be paid for the first-born, a buying back from the Lord who laid claim to all the first-born in Israel.

After the ceremony was completed, and before Mary and Joseph could find their way out of the Temple, they were halted by a complete stranger, an old man named Simeon who took the child from Mary into his own arms. Like all those who figure in the story of the early days of Our Lord's life, this man was an unknown, of no exalted office, with no claim to renown among men. He was in the Temple at this precise moment, not to exercise some priestly office but, as the Gospel so simply puts it, because he was led there by the Holy Spirit; that divinely gracious and mysterious influence which moves men, not by dragging their feet but by capturing their hearts, and floods them with joy even though the goal of the guidance be a hill and a cross. It is astonishing that Mary should have surrendered her divine child to this aged stranger without protest, that she should not have availed herself of the protecting strength of her young husband; astonishing, that is, until we recognize the kinship between this old man and this child-mother. She was full of grace, and the Holy Ghost had come upon her; the Gospel tells us of

Simeon that he was just, God-fearing, awaiting the Saviour, the Holy Ghost rested in him and had revealed to him that he would not see death until his own eyes had seen Christ the Lord. This old man and this girl were not strangers though they had never met before; the eyes of the mother of God would recognize the authentic stamp of divinity in this holy old man and her arms easily surrender the infinitely precious burden of the Son of God to him.

With the child in his arms, Simeon blessed God and set his lips to words that have ever since been an integral part of the evening prayer of the Church, words rich with all the fondness and "melancholy of an adieu":

"Now thou dost dismiss thy servant, O Lord, according to thy word in peace;
Because my eyes have seen thy salvation,
Which thou hast prepared before the face of all peoples:
A light to the revelation of the Gentiles, and the glory of thy people Israel."

The words are a farewell, but with nothing of reluctance, regret, or despair in them; this is not submission to a dismissal inevitable because there is nothing left, but rather words of parting that have an adventurous air about them, a dismissal parallel to a ship's casting off of lines to set forth for far horizons. "And His father and mother were wondering at those things which were spoken concerning Him" (Luke 2:33), and well they might. Simeon knew nothing of Gabriel's mission to Mary, of the angelic messages to Joseph and the shepherds, the revelations to Elizabeth; yet here he was divinely instructed about the Son of Mary; his words were the first hint of the world-wide character of the redemption, of salvation for the Gentiles, whom Simeon mentions indeed before the Jews. There was indeed material here for wonder. With the privilege of age, Simeon turned to Mary and Joseph and blessed them. He would already have won the heart of Mary by his obvious love of and joy in her child; now he could speak directly to her own heart outlining in his prophecy the fullness of her role of mother of the redeemer, her work of compassion, of suffering through the sufferings of her Son. "And Simeon blessed them, and said to Mary His mother: Behold this child is set for the fall, and for the resurrection of many in Israel, and for a sign which shall be contradicted; and thy own soul a sword shall pierce, that, out of many hearts, thoughts may be revealed" (Luke 2:34–35). That maternal sorrow would indeed be a sword piercing her heart, opening it wide to make of it a refuge for all the sorrowing hearts of all the ages.

This first revelation in the New Testament of the role of the Messias through the words of Simeon bore immediate fruit. Anna, a woman of some eighty-four years, did not come into the Temple, as Simeon had; she spent all her time there. She was of that class specially honored among the Romans, Jews and the early Christians, an unmarried widow, and shared Simeon's claim of sanctity's kinship with the Holy Family by her prayers, her fastings, her perpetual night and day service in the Temple; a prophetess, not in the sense of foretelling the future, but rather in the sense of adviser, counsellor, director of hearts. Her appearance beside Simeon was unlooked for, due to that same divine guidance that had brought Simeon to the spot at precisely the right moment; and her acceptance was just as complete. She shared his divinely given insight, confessed to the Lord, and became the first apostle of His Messiahship, speaking of Him to all who looked for the redemption of Israel.

The human reasons that moved Joseph to return with Mary and the child to Bethlehem instead of continuing on to Nazareth and home are not given to us by the Evangelists. The divine reasons are plain enough to us now. Three wise men from far countries were nearing Jerusalem and the end of the journey that would have been in vain if the Holy Family was not to be found in that part of the country. The journey had been undertaken, as far as men could judge, on evidence as dim as starlight, to a goal as uncertain as an undefined hope; though some of the Fathers, along with Pope Leo the Great, were sure that the feet of the wise men were guided by a greater light than the stars or the sun: "besides the outward form which aroused the attention of their corporeal eyes, a more brilliant ray enlightened their minds with the light of faith." There was ground enough for such belief, for the King Himself had without words made known His secret to Elizabeth, to Simeon, to Anna. At any rate such courage and initiative on the part of men is not in vain in the eyes of God. The Holy Family, all unknowing, in the humble tabernacle of the Cave, would be awaiting the pilgrims from the East.

An interested spectator of the arrival of these pilgrims in Jerusalem, with eyes in his head and a tongue in his mouth, could learn much of them quickly. These were men from the country east of the Dead Sea, from the land described by the vague name of Arabia, as their dress and the trappings of their journey would make plain. For all the dust and fatigue of the journey, these were grave men, men of dignity; not kings, not priests, but scholars, men set apart from other men by the sublime selflessness that is truth's gift to men who value it highly enough to search for it or hold fast to its possession. They had put hot leagues behind them and made their way into a land that was not their own for the sole purpose of seeing and paying homage to an infant king. They had, they said, but recently seen His star in the east and had come. It was as simple as that. The beckoning light of a star answered by obedience as prompt as a child's!

There were natural explanations behind such obedience, but not nearly enough. The scholarship of their country was the study of the stars that break such gaps in the night sky of the East, with particular emphasis on the attempt to divine the future of men from the course of the stars. But, as St. Chrysostom says, "It is not an astronomer's business to know from the stars those who are born, but to tell the future from the hour of a man's birth: whereas the Magi did not know the time of the birth, so as to conclude therefrom some knowledge of the future." And St. Augustine reasonably protests: "No astrologer has ever so far connected the stars with man's fate at the time of his birth as to assert that one of the stars, at the birth of any man, left its orbit and made its way to him who was just born." It was not unusual at that time for the people to see in an unknown star the sign of a new king; and it was true that the hopes and dreams of Israel had wide circulation in Arabia, wide enough to stir hopes of salvation in earnest men fighting off the despair of their world. These things are not enough to send grave men hurrying over the face of the earth to give adoration to an infant.

The star of the Magi has fascinated the minds of men from the earliest Fathers down to our most modern savants; believers or unbelievers, men simply have not been able to pass the entrancing story by without some comment. The Fathers labored with all their meditative genius and mastery of words to unveil the beauty, the mystery, the significance of the tale. In our time Science, by elaborate exhibitions in costly planetaria, points out to worshipful audiences the constellations or conjunctions of planets that took place at that time by way of showing that really nothing happened; the story was a poetic whimsy born of ignorance. It would not seem to be asking too much to demand that a man read the story before explaining it away. St. Matthew has literally excluded the possibility of a constellation or a conjunction of planets; the word he used can mean an individual, isolated star, nothing else. Moreover the story, if we are sticking to the only story we have of a starry guide to the Christ-child, demands that this individual star have movement. On this count, one might settle for a meteor or a comet as did some of the Fathers and as do some of the leading Scripture scholars of our day; but neither of these pretends that there was nothing exceptional about this meteor or comet, if it was a meteor or comet. The tale under scrutiny makes it quite plain that this movement was a guiding movement, that it brought men across the miles to such a pin-point of the world as Jerusalem, then on to the infinitesimal speck on the world's surface that was Bethlehem; indeed, even to that cave in the hillside that until this time only the native shepherds had found, and not without heavenly guidance. The hand of God was here in a special way to point out to special men a child who was God. St. Matthew has it all in the stark beauty of the Gospel's brevity: "the star which they had seen in the east went before them, until it came and stood over where the child was." A star that brings men to Jerusalem and then disappears, that reappears to lead them to Bethlehem, and then stands over a cave, its mission completed, is not to be explained by a scrutiny of the routine way of stars. The whole story of the Nativity has no meaning divorced from God, for it was God Who was born in the cave; the guiding light, moving and stopping to assure effective guidance, is an utter impossibility without God; but then the very existence of any star is no less impossible without God. With God, the story, and the world it was lived in, make sense indeed; it is the contrary stories that are the nonsense.

The arrival of the Magi in Jerusalem opened up an evening of general surprise. They themselves might well have thought that Jerusalem was the end of the work of the star, that they would no longer have to nourish their souls on slender hopes or push their quest on the motive power of stubborn faith. Arrived in the capital of the kingdom to which the great new king was born, they would reasonably expect to get all further details from almost any native; to their astonishment, everyone they accosted was astonished at their question: "Where is He that has been born, the king of the Jews?" The word of the strangers' arrival and their even stranger quest spread rapidly through the city. In no time at all the word was picked up by the agents of Herod and promptly brought to the attention of that vicious tyrant; and, as the Evangelist adds, both Herod and the people of the city were troubled by the news of the Magi. But certainly the trouble in the hearts of people and king did not have the same source. Herod's bitterly relentless violence had not lessened with the years, even though now a fatal disease gnawed at his vitals; his trouble at the word of a new-born king would be the same old trouble that had traced a trail of blood across his royal years. In his jealousy he had murdered three of his own sons, along with a host of others. It was not sympathy for Herod, nor fear of a new king that brought anxiety to the people of the royal city; rather it was that tide of uneasiness that universally floods the hearts of men in the presence of the unknown, the mysterious, or the portents of the overthrow of accustomed ways.

The people, as is the way of men over the world, would simply endure that anxiety, depending on its ultimate ebb and the consequent recovery of the comfort of routine days and unchanged ways. Herod could brook no such compromise with time; his envy, suspicion, and fear demanded instant action. His thirst for power had long since reduced the august body of the Sanhedrin to impotency, but he would not hesitate in this emergency to make use of their learning; he quickly summoned a special meeting of the learned men of that once ruling body to demand immediate information on the birthplace of the Messias as foretold by the Sacred Books. It was a tribute to the solidity of their learning and a witness to their blindness that the princes of Israel came up promptly with the one passage locating Bethlehem as the source of salvation, but did nothing with that information; it was little comfort to Herod to find both the event and its location so explicitly laid down. He could attempt to calm his fears by reminding himself of his disbelief in prophecies or of the contemptible smallness of Bethlehem; that these considerations did little to weaken his old obsession of scheming rivals is evidenced by his prompt summoning of the Magi for detailed questioning. When it became apparent to him that these grave men of the East had answered the summons of a star, that the king they sought was no more than an infant, no more than two years old by the most generously improbable calculations, and from the hamlet of Bethlehem, Herod's relief was almost ludicrously complete.

He willingly gave the wise men the answer of the prophet, showered them with presents which were much more an outlet for his relief than a gesture of courtesy, and sent them off to Bethlehem with words that were more than half patronizingly ironic: "Go and diligently inquire after the child, and when you have found Him, bring me word, that I also may come and adore Him." Only men whose own goodness made suspicion impossible could have missed the mockery of Herod's eagerness to adore a royal infant. Indeed, if Herod had taken the wise men at all seriously, they would not have been left out of sight of his agents for an instant, and they would actually have brought death to the child they came to adore, their journey's end marking the termination of the royal rule of the infant.

As it was, they set off on the path of the star, slipping out of Jerusalem unnoticed to race the last few miles to Bethlehem on feet made swift by the exceeding great joy in their hearts at the reappearance of the star. There was no delay in their departure, for what was there to hold them in Jerusalem once they had reaped the harvest of the wisdom of the prophets? In a very short time they arrived at their goal: the star stopped over the birthplace of the Saviour, and their hearts came to rest. Entering into that humble home, they found the child and Mary His mother. As was the case with the shepherds, nothing more was necessary than this very ordinary picture of a mother and her child to confirm all the wonders they had searched for: to the shepherds, this was complete confirmation of the angel's message; to the Magi, this homely scene was ultimate proof of the promise of a guiding star and a prophet's message. Both Magi and shepherds met faith's challenge triumphantly. Prostrating themselves, they worshipped Him, a gesture so common in the presence of a king at that time as to give no argument for the recognition of the divine person of the child; but a gesture totally unusual to an infant of poverty in His home in a cave, a home moreover not much less pretentious than the one He would claim through childhood in Nazareth. They worshipped Him; and so, prostrate before the child, accomplished the purpose of their long journey. Custom demanded the giving of gifts in paying homage to the great, but here it was their gratitude too that spread before the humble family the gifts typical of their country: gold, incense, and myrrh.

These gifts were symbolic, as all gifts are. Gold would be a gift fit for a king, not by its quantity but by its high place in the estimate of men as the royal metal; the incense and myrrh equally fitting as sheer luxuries, and so not to be found in the homes of the poor. Myrrh is the resin of a type of balsam tree which had astonishingly varied uses. It was a perfume particularly treasured for the scenting of clothes, it was an ingredient of a paste or lotion for hands and lips, its sweet odor was part of the flavor of funerals, and, mixed with wine, it furnished a stupefying drink deadening pain. In the eyes of the wise men, these gifts of their country were a symbolic recognition of a brilliant young king stepping into His royal future, gifts in the fullest sense of royal luxuries; there is a sharp insight here into the depth of their faith and the extent of their supernatural knowledge in the fact that they saw no incongruity in royal gifts spread out in the barrenness of a stable-cave.

The Fathers and Doctors of the Church have been fascinated by the Magi and the rich symbolism of the gifts and have probed deeply to unearth something of the divine significance so deeply imbedded in them. Thus St. Thomas makes room in the compact brevity of his Summa Theologica for loving quotation of lengthy passages. "As Chrysostom says: 'If the Magi had come in search of an earthly King, they would have been disconcerted at finding that they had taken the trouble to come such a long way for nothing. Consequently they would have neither adored nor offered gifts. But since they sought a heavenly King, though they found in Him no signs of royal pre-eminence, yet, content with the testimony of the star alone, they adored: for they saw a man, and they acknowledged a God.' Moreover, they offer gifts in keeping with Christ's greatness: 'gold, as to the great King; they offer up incense as to God, because it is used in the divine sacrifice; and myrrh, which is used in embalming the bodies of the dead, is offered as to Him Who is to die for the salvation of all' (Gregory). And hereby, as Gregory says, we are taught to offer gold, 'which signifies wisdom, to the new-born King, by the luster of our wisdom in His sight.' We offer God incense, 'which signifies fervor in prayer, if our constant prayers mount up to God with an odor of sweetness'; and we offer myrrh, 'which signifies mortification of the flesh, if we mortify the ill-deeds of the flesh by refraining from them.' "

St. Matthew closes the episode of the Magi in a few terse lines. "And having received an answer in sleep that they should not return to Herod, they went back another way into their country." To one who understands the depths of silent men, there is no implication in this that no word was spoken between the wise men and the mother of the child they had come to adore; rather, he will understand Matthew's recognition of the things that cannot be said and ought not to be stuttered about. St. Luke has told us that the shepherds rejoiced not only at what they saw but also at what they heard in the cave; and Our Lady's *Magnificat* is proof enough of the eager flood of words from her heart to those already given knowledge by God of the wonders worked in her. But Matthew is wise indeed to have attempted no paraphrase of the unfolding of the heart of the Mother of God to the wise men of the East who had come so far to share in her Son. They saw, they adored, and they heard of the wonders of Him Who was born King of the Jews and of all men; they took their rest with their hearts as full as a saint reaching up to embrace death; all the long anticipations fulfilled, hopes realized, and joy crowding their hearts.

Who, having found Mary and the child with Joseph, would want to take an immediate departure? If hope alone could drive these scholarly men so far, how willingly would the fulfillment of that hope urge their tired feet to rest here at the end of their quest! Matthew, who later left all to follow Him, would know well what it cost to leave Him; from the fullness of his knowledge, he wrote a stronger account of their living faith than the wondrous tale of obedience to a guiding star. Warned by an angel in sleep, they left what they had come so far to seek. Yet they would take more back with them than a heart can ordinarily hold; like the shepherds, they returned "praising and glorifying God, for all the things they had heard and seen, as it was told unto them." Being warned, their escape from Herod would not be difficult. By going around the southern end of the Dead Sea, or crossing it by boat, they would be on the road to home while Herod was still waiting their return to Jerusalem.

It was not for them to inquire into the reason for the angel's warning. Their grave simplicity would be slow to suspect the ruthless evil that gnawed at the heart of the king. They went their way with singing hearts to bring tidings of great joy to men of good will all along the route. It was a divine graciousness that kept them ignorant of what they had done to the Holy Family by the eager and successful quest that brought them so much rejoicing. Yet it is perfectly clear to us that the stir of their arrival in Jerusalem and the fear awakened by their search for the new-born king had torn the veil of obscurity, the staunchest protection of the poor, and unleashed the full fury of a mad king on the head of Joseph and his little family.

Very shortly after the departure of the wise men, perhaps the very next night, the warning came to Joseph to fill his heart with terror. "And after they (the wise men) were departed, behold an angel of the Lord appeared in sleep to Joseph, saying: Arise, and take the child and His mother, and fly into Egypt: and be there until I shall tell thee. For it will come to pass that Herod will seek the child to destroy Him." Joseph was plunged into this maelstrom of flight from threatened death on the heels of the peace and glory of the Magi's pilgrimage; that nocturnal warning had all the shocked suddenness of a tropical squall's almost instantaneous blocking out of the sun and uprooting of the sea. From the depths of a sleep that had been only a continuation of the tranquillity of these days at Bethlehem, he was roused to face the unchallengeable power of an oriental despot bent on the destruction of the divine child of his beloved Mary. He was a simple man, a foreigner to subtlety, far from the few humble friends of his own city, without weapons, power, wealth, or succor; yet on his shoulders rested the very life of the two who were the salvation of the world. The pressing urgency of the heavenly warning left no room for the small comfort of dallying, of minimizing the threat, of hope for some helpful intervention: arise at once, fly, a murderous king is in pursuit of a carpenter and his vagabond family. Omnipotence would work no miracles; it was precisely for this that Joseph had been given to Mary, this was Joseph's part, and it would cost him dear.

The moment his eyes were opened, he would see that the only defense open to him was the universal defense of the poor: speedy and stealthy flight. Yet how very limited even such a defense was for him; the flight could be no faster than a man could walk beside the beast that carried Mary and the child, the stages of the journey no longer than a new-born infant could support the jarring progress of the hours. In the moment it took Joseph to shake the sleep from Mary's shoulders the list of risks to be taken would mount to an account almost too much for the purse of courage to meet. They would travel alone, and so face the risks of the open road devoid of all protection. Their travel would be at night, to the exclusion of help from passing travellers; indeed the sound of hoofbeats or the scramble of steps would race their hearts and quicken the breathing of these who could expect the advent of none but enemies. The dust of the road would become sand as soon as they left the hills of Judaea, to wear down the strength of Mary by steady discomfort and threaten to choke the feeble beginnings of infant life. Perhaps the most agonizing moment of this night for Joseph's great heart was the first moment of Mary's wakefulness. Then his tongue had to be the instrument to shatter her peace and let loose the flood of terror into her sinless soul; and not a crumb of comfort to offer her beyond his love, his strength, his life. Neither could she be given even a few moments of preparation, the evil news could not be trickled gently into her mind; the warning was for her too: arise, fly, the king seeks to destroy Jesus.

There was hurry then, in the cave, almost frantic hurry, for every moment added danger to the child and every sound seemed a herald of the messengers of murder. Poverty makes short work of packing, love gives eyes to the fingers and wings to the feet. Mary would hardly have the sleep out of her eyes before she was out in the night, on the road with exile before her and death to the child on her heels; but with Joseph at her side to take care both of the exile and the enemies. The silent Matthew has given us an accurate estimate of the caliber of Joseph, and of Mary's love for the carpenter in his almost laconic account of Joseph's response to the angelic warning: "Who [Joseph] arose, and took the child and His mother by night, and retired into Egypt." Just so do simple men rise simply to the heroic; just so does love respond, discarding the delay of questions.

Had not the frenzy of his anger so blurred the mind of King Herod, the Holy Family would easily have been destroyed and the night they sought as a refuge would have cloaked the crime by which they were obliterated. Certainly, the departure of the wise men towards the East was no secret in Bethlehem, nor could it have been, granted the size of Bethlehem, the tongues and trappings of the foreigners, the penetrating curiosity and the light regard for privacy common in the East. Herod knew quickly that these strangers had flouted his invitation to return, disregarded his royal commands. This was more than enough to fire the anger of a despot; his almost insane fear of rivals for his throne fanned that fire to a raging blaze. He struck out with a brutality so blind as to defeat his murderous purpose. A force, sufficient to overwhelm the desperation of mothers and the helpless courage of fathers defending the lives of their babies, was instantly dispatched to Bethlehem to kill every male child of two years and under. Herod's computation of time went far beyond the information he had received from the Magi, to make sure beyond all mistake that this threatened rivalry of an infant be eliminated; yet a few inquiries would have revealed the departure of the Holy Family, they could not have been long on the road, and the pace they set would be no match for the speed of the king's horsemen. But no; blindly, brutally, in insensate anger, some twenty infants, all that the village of Bethlehem had to offer to the sword of royalty, were snatched from their mothers and openly butchered. Human life was cheap to the Oriental tyrant, particularly where there was no threat of reprisal; the bloody deed easily finds historical parallels and on a far larger scale. But this does not make the running blood less red, nor the arms of weeping mothers less empty; perhaps we get the full flavor of the horror of this deed if we remember that infants were kept at the breast for well up to two years—a massacre, then, of sucklings. This brave bold deed of the king's horsemen gave us the first martyrs for Christ; the Holy Innocents who testified with their blood before their tongues could speak.

Meanwhile the Holy Family hurried through the

night towards Egypt and safety. A steady journey of five or six hours would bring them over the borders of the Roman Province of Egypt, and so out of Herod's power. Not a long journey ordinarily but hours are shortened by happiness, lengthened by misery, and stretched to intolerable lengths when the terror of catastrophe haunts every passing second. Only Joseph could tell how dreadfully long that night's journey was. His complete faith, prompt obedience, and prudent haste brought Mary and the child to safety. Crossing the border, they could breathe again, pause for some badly needed rest, and realize, as taut nerves relaxed, how much of their lives had been burnt up in that race from the wrath of a king. The young wife's love and complete faith in her husband protected Mary from the worst of fear's fierce assaults; now, with physical safety wrapping her about like the walls of a home, she could give her full attention to the child and leave the details of the immediate future to Joseph.

For Joseph, the successful escape from Herod merely opened the door to a new set of anxieties. Here he was, with Mary and the child, in a land whose tongue was strange to him, the customs as foreign as the tongue, the very cast of the features of the people he met emphasizing the frightening fact of his exile. In this strange land, it was Joseph's work to find shelter and a livelihood for a time as indefinite as the angel's words: "be there until I shall tell thee." He had the gold of the Magi and his own two hands, and all the reasons for uncertainty that crowd the mind of a humble man who knows so honestly the narrow limits of his own powers. Joseph was the support of Mary and the child in the full, solid sense of that word: a firm foundation, a pillar of strength, a stout wall of defense, a secure source of nourishment.

Standing on his own two feet, he met all the threats the world can make to the family of a man, met them and hurled them back. This is the work of a father, a work that must be done alone, not shared with the family; here a man, under God, plays the role of God with fear and loneliness constantly testing his courage and unselfish love.

We know that the Holy Family had to travel only five or six hours from Bethlehem to achieve safety in Egypt; how far they had to penetrate that land to secure a livelihood we do not know. We have no knowledge of the city, town or hamlet that sheltered them during their stay in Egypt. Naturally, they would gravitate towards one or another of the Jewish colonies where, at least, they could make themselves understood and be told of opportunities for the use of Joseph's skill at his craft. Joseph had to make long-range plans, for he had no notion as to the length of his exile. In actual fact, that exile was not to last longer than some weeks or at most some months. Herod did not long survive the sucklings he had murdered, and it was the death of the enemy of the infant that was to mark the end of the Egyptian exile and the beginning of the trek homeward.

"But when Herod was dead, behold an angel of the Lord appeared in sleep to Joseph in Egypt, saying: Arise and take the child and His mother, and go into the land of Israel. For they are dead that sought the life of the child. Who arose, and took the child and His mother, and came into the land of Israel." There are no bright visions for Joseph, always the shadows; it is in sleep that he receives the angelic messages. Always the phrases are the same: Mary and the child, the child and His mother; underlining both the virginity of Mary and the minor role of guardian given to Joseph. And always, his faith and obedience are prompt, unquestioning, almost matter of fact. This, at least, was one journey which Mary and Joseph could approach with gay hearts, and not a worry in the world; they were going home. The memory of that first journey, under the pressure of the Roman census and with Mary's time approaching, of the hurry and awful fright of the journey to Egypt, these would only heighten the bright prospects of this return to home.

All the miles were short, and all the hours fast as they climbed to the hill country of Judaea; and days could be packed with plans, and dreams, and tenderness. Crossing back into their native land, Joseph would shortly hear of the violence of the new king, Archelaus, the worst of the sons of Herod, who had with brutal finality just ended a threat of civil war. Joseph had had enough of murderous kings. "But hearing that Archelaus reigned in Judaea in the room of Herod his father, he was afraid to go thither: and being warned in sleep retired into the quarters of Galilee. And coming he dwelt in a city called Nazareth: that it might be fulfilled which was said by the prophets: That He shall be called a Nazarene." Home again, and all the quiet years stretching out before them.

4

NAZARETH'S THIRTY YEARS

MARY'S days in Nazareth were no different exteriorly from those of the other women of the town. Her child was only a few months old when she arrived back home with Joseph. She would, then, necessarily be lavishing on the child a mother's ceaseless care of its helplessness: anticipating the child's needs, interpreting its protests, protecting it from discomforts. Through all this there would echo that joy that forever remains a woman's secret knowledge, a closeness to one so dear that finds its climax and most touching physical expression as the child draws nourishment and growth directly from the mother's breast.

Since the departure for Bethlehem so long ago, the paralysis induced by disuse had gripped their little home; but it would not take long for Mary to cure that deadly dullness in a house of two rooms with furniture limited to a table, a few stools, a cabinet or two, and a low bedstead with its wool or sheepskin blanket. Her household tasks were for the most part not those of our day. There was the grain to grind into flour with the rough mill of two specially shaped stones; the oil to prepare from olives; bread to bake in the little outdoor oven; cheese and wine to make; honey and such fruits as figs, dates, grapes to gather or to purchase. Little more than this found its way to their frugal table; perhaps some salted fish in the evening at the principal meal, but rarely if ever would they have meat. In between times there was the wool to spin and the garments for the whole family to weave. There was the endless round of washing, mending, cleaning; and the perpetual job of the portage of water from the town's well. The sharp difference between Our Lady and her contemporaries stemmed from the double root of her crystalline sanctity and her motherly closeness to God. In all of her day, she had the Son of God under her eyes and uppermost in her heart. Moment by moment, day by day, it became more overwhelmingly clear to the eyes of Joseph that his humble house sheltered more sanctity than the world would ever see in any other age; his house was the home of God and His mother.

Joseph's home would be his refuge in the evenings and on holidays; for the rest, like most men, he would spend his days at his trade, and the artisans of his day did not have their shops in their own homes. Mary and the child would have the house to themselves for the long length of the working day, while Joseph ruled over the shop. His work demanded and developed strong hands and arms, broad shoulders, as well as the craftsman's smoothly sure hands and an eye for the perfection of line, plane, angle; for the true artisan detects the hidden beauty in rough material and unveils it with a skillfulness that is not far from tenderness. The carpenters of Joseph's time worked directly on the trees and logs bought from woodcutters. From these they fashioned farm implements such as plows, yokes, handles for farm tools; the household furniture of stools, tables, cabinets, beds; the beams that would frame the roof of the buildings, its window frames and doors. Their tools were extensions for clever hands and strong arms, not mechanical substitutions for eye, arms, and hands; for the most part they would be limited to the plane, axe, saw, hammer, mallet and chisel. This was work for a strong and patient man, one who had respect for the living wood on which he worked and a justified pride in the perfection of the work of his hands.

Joseph's was a sociable profession. The men of the towns and the farms were his customers, not heavily endowed with money and therefore cautious and thorough, unhurried in their transactions; relaxed and pleasantly social when the deal was completed, caught too by the fascination of the unskilled for the craftsman's artistry. There would be so many things to talk of before and after: the qualities of different woods, sizes and shapes, durability and beauty, time's testing of older products, evaluations of competing artisans, and so on; there was always, of course, the matter of crops, weather, politics, the Greeks and the Romans, as well as the news of families and individuals that could be had in no other way than this familiar interchange that ties townspeople so closely together. The surroundings in which Joseph spent his day would add an extra flavor to the joy with which he returned in the evening to the most womanly of women and the helplessness of the infant.

Joseph's trade was sociable in a much wider sense than the easy camaraderie of the shop itself. He and the boy who would succeed him as the carpenter of Nazareth did not have their days imprisoned within the walls of a shop and a home; they would know well, and be known by, people over a fairly wide range of territory. The repair of plows, yokes, and so on would take the carpenter out to the small farms; the work on buildings would take him to the neighboring towns, perhaps even to the great cities of Sephoris and Tiberias, three and sixteen miles away; the labor on home furnishings would take him into homes of both the rich and the poor. To a man as quietly wise as Joseph, with his tongue offering no competition to the outpourings of others and his eyes penetrating to the deep wells behind the flow of words, this daily labor in the homes, on the farms, in the bustling activity of men, would be a school which taught well all the appealing complexities of the hearts of men and women: the pride, courage, the fears, the plans, the dashed hopes and fading dreams all knit together by the loves that make or mar the lives they dominate. To the divinely wise son of the carpenter, taking up this labor in His turn, the days would be a constant theater for the play of divine gentleness, understanding, and mercy long before it was time for His divinity to be made known to men. The rough edges of the lives of the men and women of Nazareth would be planed to smoothness by the carpenter and his family though they never realized the unobtrusivc helpfulness that protected them. The hidden life does not mean that Mary, Jesus and Joseph retired into isolated privacy; it means only that the divinity of Our Lord received no outward manifestation and that history has hidden from us the details of the lives that flowed so generously into the lives of their contemporaries in Nazareth.

The end of the long day's labors would bring Mary and Joseph together, grateful for the respite of the cool quiet of the evening. In warm weather, those precious hours of family intimacy that give meaning to all the rest of the day would be spent on the flat top of the little house, the beauty of plain and mountains spread out as gifts of the beneficent God, the clear closeness of the sky a reminder of His protecting love. It was then that Joseph would be told of the child's day, for Mary would hardly hide from him the details so dear to Joseph's fatherly love; indeed her own heart would look forward to these hours which offered her the only opportunity in all the long day to release the pent-up joy and love of her own heart. There was no other in all Nazareth but Joseph who shared the King's secret, and it was not Mary's to make that secret known. These are the hours, consecrated by the utterly unselfish and mutual love of the child, that open the eyes of husband and wife to the heights of nobility in each other, the hours, then, for the deepening, widening, heightening of the mutual love that makes them one. To Joseph here in the evening, Mary's flaming sanctity would light up her every act, her smiles, her least gesture, her face in repose, to make of them a fire warming a man to his very depths and spurring him on to much more than his very best; while the quiet strength, the patient routine, the unobtrusive labors of Joseph would make more plain to Mary the fineness of the man and the reckless generosity of his love, more plain even than in the days of her espousals, of Bethlehem, and of Egypt.

Physically, Nazareth was ideal for the childhood of the Saviour. The eye avid for beauty could hardly find a better vantage point, for Nazareth was caught up between plains and mountains, between lake and sea. Looking south, the rich plain of Esdrelon spread out at one's feet studded with towns like a rich carpet of intricate design; to the north, the mountains towered over the puny height that seemed so majestic from the level of the plain. To the west on a clear day there was the dim blue of the Mediterranean, while to the east, clear and sparkling at its sixteen miles distance, was the lake of Tiberias. Nazareth escaped both the tropical heat of the plains it dominated, and the fierce cold of the mountains in whose protecting shadows it relaxed in confident security. The countryside round about was a garden spot of fertility. It was a retired town, by no means isolated, but like a quiet street just off a busy thoroughfare; main caravan routes both north and south, and east and west ran almost by its door. Its neighborhood was crowded with little towns no larger and just as unimportant as Nazareth itself, while nearby were such flourishing cities as Sephoris and Tiberias, both royally built and endowed.

On the other hand, the Galilee of Nazareth was a dangerous place. Its physical advantages and abundant opportunities inevitably attracted the Gentiles. Exchange, banking, and much of the commerce were mainly in the hands of the Greeks; the Romans were the large property owners, with the natives largely tenants and slaves. The flourishing markets were a steady enticement to all the excesses of avarice with its contempt for men. The court of Herod Antipas, son of the Herod who had murdered the children of Bethlehem, was a centre of sensual corruption; the low, often perverse, estimate of religion removed all restraint from the pagan license of Greeks and Romans. To God-fearing Jews, every day carried multiple threats of this foul contamination spreading to their homes and their families. Already renowned for the careful discipline and religious education they gave to their children, under this threat from the pagan despoilers of their native land the Jews of Galilee redoubled the care exercised on their rearing. The synagogue and the home were the only weapons at hand to hold the contaminating flood at bay and they made the utmost use of these two safeguards.

The peace in the home of Joseph was divinely abundant, absolutely unmarred; and Nazareth itself, by its very obscurity, was given a generous portion of peace. But the early years of Our Lord's life were by no means peaceful years in Galilee. The death of Herod the Great, which signalled the end of the exile in Egypt, was also the signal for political uproars throughout the whole land. Just about the time the Holy Family returned to Nazareth, Sephoris, then the chief city of Galilee, had been attacked by the rebel Judas; in retaliation, it was stormed by the Roman Varus, burnt to the ground, and all its inhabitants enslaved. In smothering the fires of that insurrection, Varus had two thousand captives crucified. Ten years later, the countryside was persistently upset by the intense resistance to the Romans by Judas the Galilean with his band of zealots. The splendor of royal ambitions built the city of Tiberias, and later rebuilt in new glory the destroyed Sephoris; this same weak, voluptuous ruler, later the murderer of John the Baptist in defense of his own incest, steadily added infection to the thoroughly diseased morals of his province. The pagans themselves were committed to philosophies of despair, their religions adding nothing but more reasons for despair; while the political slavery of the Jews and the thorough exploitation they suffered at the hands of their conquerors left them no hope but in the age-long promise of the Messias. The very air was contaminated with pagan ideas and pagan ideals, heavy with despair. The only remedy offered was distraction, and a type of distraction that fed the despair to new fatness: Sephoris and Tiberias had theatres for Greek plays, amphitheatres for pagan games and sports, and there were religious festivals for the complete debasement of men and women, their love, and their marriage.

In this Galilee of the Gentiles, in the obscurity of Nazareth, in the holy peace of the little house of the carpenter, the divine child passed from infancy, through childhood, to sturdy boyhood with nothing of the miraculous to single Him out from children of the same age in Nazareth. St. Luke sums up the first twelve years of that life in just two lines that, for all their compressed brevity, make clear the parallel development of body and mind, the physical health and strength of the child, and the good pleasure of God in this masterpiece of humanity that yet was God. "And the child grew and waxed strong, filled with wisdom, and the grace of God was in Him" (Luke 2:40). With none of the inheritance of weakness which is the fruit of original sin, for He had no human father to transmit Adam's seed and His mother was immaculately conceived, the child's life began in physical perfection. The disciplined simplicity, which necessity imposes on the poor, added to the early sharing of labors which is both the boon and the burden of the poor, leaves us with no grounds for fantastic conceptions of the son of Mary as delicate, somewhat feminine, moving fragilely through perfumed days. This child grew, He became big; His strength was such as to be worth explicit mention in a document sparing of words; a big, strong boy with a promise of early usefulness in the strenuous labors of the carpenter shop. From the beginning, Christ had God's knowledge, for He was God; He had the knowledge that comes to the mind of man from the vision of God, for He had that vision; He had the knowledge that is the fruit of infused ideas, a consequent of the state of the blessed. Despite all this, the child, day by day, was filled with wisdom; He had a human intellect that would have been possessed in vain if it did not reap the rich harvest of knowledge hidden in the inanimate world about Him, in plants and animals, in the faces, the words, the actions of men and women. There was real growth here, growth of body and mind, for Jesus Christ was truly man.

If they could have afforded it, the Holy Family would have gone to Jerusalem three times a year in obedience to the command of the law. In actual fact, the length of the journey, their poverty, and the necessary interruption of Joseph's labors limited them to the single annual pilgrimage for the great feast of the Pasch. But every year, and probably not without some considerable sacrifice and planning, they went the long way to Jerusalem: "And His parents went every year to Jerusalem at the solemn day of the Pasch" (Luke 2:41). This was not only a personal privilege, it was a religious duty joyously done by these three who were so close to God. Most of their townsfolk who could arrange it at all would also make the pilgrimage; indeed, they would travel as a town group, men, women and children together, picking up other similar groups as they made their way south. The law did not oblige the women and children to attendance at these feasts in Jerusalem, but of course they would go whenever it was possible. Mary and Joseph were not separated in this affair, as they were not in any other; so year after year they went up to the Holy City with the divine child.

One of these pilgrimages is singled out by St. Luke for detailed treatment; there, drawing on the memory of Our Lady, he gives us the only details we have of the young years of God's Son made man. At the time of this particular pilgrimage, Mary was twenty-six or twenty-seven years old, in the full bloom of her young beauty; Joseph was in his early thirties, about the age that St. Thomas considered the perfect age of full maturity; the divine child was twelve, precisely at that age where the law would hold Him more strictly responsible and where He would be expected to begin the commanded fasts. "And when he was twelve years old, they going up into Jerusalem, according to the custom of the feast, and having fulfilled the days, when they returned, the child Jesus remained in Jerusalem, and His parents knew it not." Mary and Joseph lost the divine child! Only after three days of separation did they find Him. The mystery of that agonized separation, and the even greater mystery of their recovery of the boy, are swords opening the heart of Mary for all the world and slitting just a little the veil that still hid the redemptive mission of the Son of God.

"Thinking He was in the company, they came a day's journey, and sought Him among their kinsfolk and acquaintance, and not finding Him, they returned into Jerusalem, seeking Him" (Luke 2:44–45). There was no carelessness on the part of Mary and Joseph. Jesus had been in Jerusalem each year; He knew well the return routine of the caravans, their starting time and departure point. Ordinarily the start would be rather late in the day, and a straggling sort of thing; not everyone would leave at exactly the same time and the first day's journeying would be only some three or four hours. It was at that first stopping point that the different town groups would be firmly gathered together and continue on, the next day, in the same family fashion in which they had come to the feast. The thing could not have happened if Mary had been a selfish, nagging mother refusing to let her child grow up; or if Jesus was an irresponsible or recalcitrant child whom Joseph would not dare to let out of his sight for fear of what

He might do next. Since Mary was a wise and generous mother, she would give more and more liberty to her perfect son as His years merited it; Joseph would know from the years past how completely trustworthy and responsible Jesus was. All the circumstances heavily underline the completely deliberate character of the boy's delay in Jerusalem, and so point clearly to the divine significance of the things done and said, as well as of the pain inflicted on Mary and Joseph.

Every parent can see something of the anxiety that began to seep into the hearts of Mary and Joseph as night fell on the caravan at rest. They would have noticed the absence of the child as they left Jerusalem, but with no uneasiness; supposing of course that He would catch up with them in the course of the day's short travel. As they got closer to the place where they would rest for the night, they began to look more alertly, and alertness would soon find room for worry. When a thorough canvass of the Nazareth group failed to find the child, terror would have gained a foothold within them. Once night had fallen, there was nothing to be done beyond trying to ride out the storm of fears, self-accusations, and heartsick misery that stretched the hours of the night to interminable lengths. The words of comfort and reassurance Mary and Joseph would offer each other during the night would be empty, sterile things, for there was neither comfort nor reassurance in either heart to be shared. Joseph, the protector and guardian, had not failed to find shelter in Bethlehem, he had not failed against kings and exile, he had not failed in the daily routine of Nazareth; but here his simple honesty could not evade the bitter truth, here he had failed, failed both the child and his beloved Mary. Since she had declared herself the handmaid of the Lord to Gabriel, this was the first time Mary had been separated from her God-given son; handmaid, servant, slave wholly dedicated to Him—and she had lost Him. In later years, she would return from Calvary to an empty Jerusalem; but it would not be nearly as devastatingly empty as was the world on this night. No human heart had comfort enough to assuage the anguish of Joseph and Mary on this first night since Bethlehem that they had been alone.

Early in the morning, the second day of their desolate separation from Jesus, Mary and Joseph took the road back towards Jerusalem; short as the distance was, it was a long, increasingly anxious road. Again and again they would meet groups of pilgrims homeward bound, and each time their eager search and hopefully exhaustive inquiries met only ignorance: no, the child was not in the group, no, no one had seen a boy answering this description, perhaps He was with the group just behind. So it went through the length of the day, with hope's flame dying down to a flickering ember. The second night of anguish left no room for even the pretense of comfort or reassurance; these two who knew each other so well could not hope to hide their suffering, the dimming of their hope. Yet each would know that the other would not fail from lack of courage or stubborn faith. It would need such courage and faith to press the search for a boy alone in the maze of Jerusalem's streets and the press of its teeming population.

Meanwhile Jesus had spent His hours "in the temple, sitting in the midst of the doctors, hearing them and asking them questions" (Luke 2:46). As St. Luke draws the picture, it is not the painting of a bright boy interrupting the master's lecture and thus drawing attention to his precocious brilliance. The usual lecture was carried on by a single master seated on a bench while his students grouped about him sitting on mats on the floor. The case here was of a group of these masters talking among themselves, perhaps centered upon some one of them of peculiar authority and learning. There would be no feeling whatever against a boy listening in on the edge of such a group; as a matter of fact, it would be entirely normal procedure for one of the masters to draw the boy into the discussion smilingly, for it was a real delight to the doctors of Israel to discover and cultivate the future masters of Israel; then, too, where there is real mastery, there is no need to defend uncertainty and weakness by standing aloof on dignity rather than walking serenely on truth. The personal charm of this big, strong boy with so much of character and intelligence in His face attracted still greater attention to His answers; remember, too, the real scholar's quick respect for an earnest mind, however youthful, the pride of race in the doctors which would give them a proprietary, almost a paternal, claim to His excellence, the conquering charm of youthful perfection that later on, in its maturity, would clog the roads of Palestine and crowd its deserts. This does not by any means explain the progress of these discussions; "And all that heard Him were astonished at His wisdom and His answers." The word used here means extreme astonishment, not terror, or stupefaction, but open-mouthed wonder such as grips a man seeing a miracle worked under his very eyes. The amazement in both cases, at the doctrine and the miracles, is traceable to the same source: supernatural power unveiled before the eyes of men. Here, for a short time, the Son of God allowed the wisdom that was His as God to be put to the lowly task of answering the questions of men. It was not a bright boy but the living God that held the masters of Israel amazed.

With steps slowed by the burden of heavy hearts, Mary and Joseph came to the temple on the third day and their eyes, dull from lack of sleep and too much searching, fell upon this scene; almost, they refused to believe their eyes. "They were struck with wonder," with a wonder even greater than the amazement of the masters of Israel. It was not only the thunderclap of joy that reverberated through their whole beings at the successful end of their almost hopeless search; for twelve years they had lived with this child, knowing well His divine origins, but with no slightest word or action to disturb the pattern of ordinary, routine, natural development of a human child. Yet here was divine wisdom flowing from His lips to refresh the parched souls of the greatest in Israel! The human heart does not take casually the vivid reminder that it harbors omnipotence.

However great the impact of joy and the shock of divinity at work, they were not enough to smother the motherly instincts of Our Lady. Mary's response to the situation was so authentically maternal and so generously domestic as to make all future mothers and fathers her willing slaves. "And His mother said to Him: Son, why hast thou done so to us? behold thy father and I have sought thee sorrowing." A mother's heart, suddenly freed of the choking bonds of fears and anxieties, leaps up in a surge of relief that universally finds expression in an exasperated rebuke; here, Mary let her heart take charge despite the sacred precincts of the temple, the awesome presence of the doctors, and the divinity of her son. Yet even at such a moment, her own sorrow is relegated to a second place in her concern for the sorrow of another; all through the anxious three days, the sorrow of Joseph was uppermost in her mind, as Mary's was in his; her words place him first, for her great love has penetrated the depths of his sorrow and the sharpness of relief is for him first, her rebuke for the pain that was thrust on the heart of this loved one by the failure of his guardianship.

If our blindness can see so much of beauty, of generosity, of love in Mary's words, how greatly must they have been treasured by the divine wisdom of her Son who saw all of her heart! We must keep this well in mind if we are to escape a misunderstanding of the response of Jesus. "And He said to them, 'How is it that you sought Me? did you not know that I must be about My father's business?' " Here was no rebuke of Mary but an affair where costs are not to be counted, the same affair that later did not spare the heart of the Blessed Mother on Calvary. His father's business, His eternal Father, was to teach men truth, to give them the life of grace, to die for their sins; before that, every human consideration must give way. The answer of Jesus may seem severe to a casual reader: these two had not doubted His divine mission, they had not placed impediments in its way, they had made no demands upon Him. In reality, the answer was not severe but profound; probably the Fathers had it right when they saw Jesus smiling upon His mother as He answered her. Certainly it was as profound, not as severe, that Mary took His words. "And they understood not the word that He spoke unto them. . . . And His mother kept all these words in her heart." This was her initiation into the heartaches of the redemption of men, the only share Joseph would have in those sorrows; here was another plunge into still deeper darkness of faith. The words were not understood, indeed all of a lifetime in her heart would not serve to exhaust them, for they reached to divine horizons. It was enough for Mary and Joseph to accept the words, to have the child again with them, and to have the quiet to keep the words in their hearts.

There was no quarrel here, no hurt feelings, only joyous reunion. "And He went down with them, and came to Nazareth, and was subject to them. . . . And Jesus advanced in wisdom, and stature,* and grace with God and men." Thus St. Luke signals the return to the routine of family life after this one flash of divinity. In these few words he sums up the long eighteen years that stretched from this moment to the Lord's departure from Nazareth to take up His public life at the age of thirty. Again there is special stress laid on the physical and mental development of the son of Mary, on the size and strength of His body, the busy activity of His mind, and the winning charm that captivated both God and men. As the years unfolded their routine of daily labor and poverty's pinched planning, they took a heavy toll of Mary's youth; as her boy marched up the hill of the years to His full stature, His mother went step by step down the other side into middle age. Yet, remembering the leaping progress of her heart towards God, we are right in our picture of her as ever young, for each year she would be closer to the source of life, nearer to the eternal springtime of the soul, steadily approaching eternal beginnings; there would be no lessening of the gaiety of her heart, the light of her smile, the joy of her eyes, whatever the years did to the strength of her hands or the quickness of her step.

Some time during this span of eighteen years, Joseph died. We could argue that the providence of God would not put an end to Joseph's fatherly protection of mother

* Douay version, *Age*.

and child until the boy had reached an age where He could take on the daily labors on which that little home depended; on the other hand, the descriptions of Jesus later as the "Son of Mary" and the "carpenter of Nazareth" vaguely indicate that Joseph had been dead long enough by the time Jesus was thirty years old for the memory of him to blur in the minds of his townsfolk. Actually, we have no historical details. We can see in this death of Joseph a divine limitation of his part in the work of redemption, dismissing him when need for him ended as he had been introduced into it only when necessity had demanded; another emphasis of the obscure place that was Joseph's, in the shadows. We can see his death as a divine mercy sparing him the full share he would otherwise have in the sorrows of Mary and Jesus; or a divine precaution not exposing the indignant strength of a quiet man to a provocation that could not be borne without a violent rush to the defense of his loved ones. But it is futile for the mind of man to attempt to read the plans of God. What we can know beyond all question is the gap that was left in that little home, and in the heart of Mary, by the death of Joseph; we can know to what great waves of sorrow the heart of Mary was exposed in her later years by the absence of the strong comfort of Joseph's love; and Joseph's long wait amid the shadows of limbo. It is clear that Mary was to be spared no sorrow, to be given no reprieve, that all sorrowing hearts might find refuge and understanding in her. We can understand too that the full burden of work at the carpenter's craft would be the final contribution to the rugged strength of Mary's Son, hardening His hands, tempering the fine steel of His endurance, bestowing resources of strength on arms and legs; He would need every ounce of that strength in a mission that often enough allowed not so much as time to eat, a mission that after three exhausting years would demand a slow, agonized death without murmur or complaint.

The years flowed quietly by in Nazareth. The shadow of the cross grew more distinct over the home of the carpenter and His mother. Finally, the days of preparation were finished. One day He set out in earnest about His Father's business; Mary's farewell would be said uncomplainingly but the sword would not cut less deep into her heart for all her willing silence. The years had been long and packed tight with joy since Gabriel had come to the child Mary of Nazareth. Now her arms were emptier than her home. The thirty years of Nazareth were over; but their passing did not change the response of the virgin: "behold the handmaid of the Lord; be it done unto me according to thy word."

5

DAWN OF SALVATION

TWO Galilean fishermen, Andrew and John, stood on the high banks of the deep-cutting Jordan; not far to the south, the river emptied itself fruitlessly into the Dead Sea as though in hopeless surrender to the desolate aridity of the area to which its sunken waters brought no fertility. As they stood there with John the Baptist, the son of Elizabeth and Zachary, Jesus passed by. "And beholding Jesus walking, he (John) saith: 'Behold the Lamb of God.' And the two disciples heard him speak, and they followed Jesus. And Jesus turning and seeing them following Him, saith to them 'What seek ye?' Who said to Him, 'Rabbi' (which is to say, being interpreted, master,) 'where dwellest thou?' He saith to them: 'Come and see.' They came, and saw where He abode, and they stayed with Him that day; now it was about the tenth hour" (John 1:36–39).

For the first time the Son of Mary is looked on by men with an interest, fanned by hope, as something more than the Carpenter of Nazareth. The light was beginning to be cast on the world, but as gently, as gradually as the almost imperceptible coming of dawn. The interest of these two fiery men of a Galilee traditionally violent was not lighted by a blaze of glory sweeping across their horizons; there were deep human roots to this interest though its final fruits were to be so thoroughly divine. There was no mystery in the presence of Galileans about the Jordan at this time. A voice had been heard in the land that would have drawn Galileans from the ends of the earth; a message had been delivered that would electrify every sincere son of Israel; a man had come from the deserts to shatter the centuries-long silence of the prophets by the terrible authenticity of his recall of men to God. The voice was heard in the wilderness, but it echoed throughout the land.

It was in October or November of the year A.D. 27, that, at the word of God, John, the son of Zachary, had come from the desert southeast of Jerusalem. There he had spent his formative years in rigid austerity, his diet locusts and wild honey, his clothes a camel's hair garment and a leathern girdle; now, the perfectly tuned instrument of divinity, he stood before men in a strength of soul that struck out at men through a body that offered no hindrance to the divine purposes consuming the man. "Do penance," he said, "for the kingdom of heaven is at hand." "For this is he that was spoken of by Isaias the prophet, saying: 'A voice of one crying in the desert, Prepare ye the way of the Lord, make straight His paths' " (Matt. 3:2–3).

The nation reeled under his words, then rallied to rush to this last of the prophets. Men had waited so long for this word. Sorrow and danger had so crowded the hearts of men that there was barely room for hope. The national tragedy of subjection to a foreigner was surpassed by the pagan travesties and profanations of religion which seeped through all the land; inevitably the moral decay made its insistent threat. Men of good will remembered the promise of the prophets, hoped against the weight of time, and listened desperately for the promised precursor of the Messias. Now this voice came from the wilderness; and it would be hard for sincere men to doubt that this was indeed the long-waited prophet. He thundered for the reform of the individual, demanding confession of sins as the sign of contrition and baptizing in the rivulets running in steep furrows to join the Jordan; a new rite, indeed, but with the familiar note of purification as a symbol of spiritual cleanness. Reform, personal reform, fruits worthy of penance. These are hard things; the Sadducees and Pharisees in the crowd would be laggard, as leaders often are in following, and at them John unleashed the full fury of his zeal for the people looking to them for guidance. "Ye brood of vipers, who hath shewed you to flee from the wrath to come? Bring forth therefore fruit worthy of penance. And think not to say within yourselves, we have Abraham for our father. For I tell you that God is able of these stones to raise up children to Abraham. For now the axe is laid to the root of the trees. Every tree therefore that doth not yield good fruit, shall be cut down, and cast into the fire" (Matt. 3:7–10).

There was pity in the very violence with which he warned of the wrath of God's judgments; he was concerned with mercy to men. The gentle kindliness of the strong, who need none of those exhibitions of strength which hide weakness and its fears, wove a spell about the people even greater than the uncompromising denunciations that rang from his lips. The penitent publicans could have approached any class in all Israel and have been met with no more than a scathing condemnation. These universally despised and hated gougers of their own people came to John to ask in humble simplicity: "Master, what are we to do?" They were met by a mildness as delicate as a mother's and given a command tempered to a minimum by a charity as unberstanding as it was divine: "Exact no more than what has been appointed you" (Luke 3:13). The soldiers, really police agents who compelled the recalcitrant to pay the exorbitant taxes, met no heroic challenges, were burdened by no blistering rebukes: "Plunder no man," said John, "neither accuse anyone falsely, and be content with your pay" (Luke 3:14). Mercy is more startling than might, and rarer among men. It was no wonder that "the people were in expectation, and all were wondering in their hearts about John, whether perhaps he might be the Christ" (Luke 3:15). In later years, it would be clear how truly John foreshadowed the Master he had come to announce.

There was nothing of self in John's mission, nothing but mercy that could not brook the unkindness of deceit, even self-deceit. He made his mission plain, shouting it for all to hear: "There cometh after me one mightier than I, the latchet of whose shoes I am not worthy to stoop down and loose. I have baptized you with water; but He shall baptize you with the Holy Ghost" (Mark 1:7–8). "Whose fan is in His hand, and He will purge His floor, and will gather the wheat into His barn; but the chaff He will burn with unquenchable fire" (Luke 3:17). His mission was plain. He was the precursor, the forerunner, the voice in the wilderness crying out to men to prepare their hearts for the coming of the reign of the Lord. Here was a prophet, indeed, the greatest of the prophets; the people flocked to him, and with him waited. It was time for the Lord.

The excitement of John's appearance and message had long since spread to Galilee, finding its way more quickly into the humble homes that had waited and prayed so earnestly for a Saviour; in none of those humble houses did the word pierce more deeply into human hearts than in the Carpenter's home in Nazareth. They, too, had waited, Jesus and Mary, waited with all love's eager willingness and all of nature's dread; it was not yet time for the agony of Gethsemani, but something of its bitterness was here in the first sip of the cup. Jesus did not at once leave Galilee in response to the precursor's preaching; the way had first to be prepared, the baptizing and preaching of John to be well under way, the hearts of men to be brought to readiness. Indeed, it was not until about January that he left the shadows of Nazareth for the glare of the roads and the beginning of his bid for the hearts and the happiness of men.

"Then cometh Jesus from Galilee to the Jordan, unto John, to be baptized by him" (Matt. 3:13). The Fathers found many a reason for the Messias submitting himself to the baptism of his precursor. Thus St. Ambrose: "This is justice, to do first thyself that which thou wishest another to do, and so encourage others by thy example." "Our Lord was baptized because He wished, not to be cleansed, but to cleanse the waters, that, being purified by the flesh of Christ that knew no sin, they might have the virtue of baptism." "Let none decline the laver of grace, since Christ did not refuse the laver of penance." There was John's work to be confirmed and the waters of the world to be cleansed for that baptism by the Holy Ghost of which John had spoken. As Christ descended into the waters to be baptized, He came as a total stranger to his cousin, the Baptist; the latter acknowledged later that "he did not know Him." John had been the first to recognize the Son of Mary while both were still in the womb; but now, face to face, the Carpenter was a stranger to the Baptist, for the Son of God is not to be recognized by the eyes of the body but through the gift of God, through the eyes of faith. Yet here, in this confrontation in the Jordan, we have again that mysterious recognition of sanctity by a saint. The sinless John, sanctified in the womb of his mother and ignorant of the divinity of this man who stood before him, drew back as though he himself were unclean before such sanctity. "But John stayed him, saying: 'I ought to be baptized by thee, and comest thou to me?' And Jesus answering, said to him: 'Suffer it to be so now. For so it becometh us to fulfill all justice.' Then he suffered Him" (Matt. 3:14–15).

"When all the people were baptized, Jesus also being baptized and praying, heaven was opened; And the Holy Ghost descended in a bodily shape, as a dove upon Him; and a voice came from heaven: Thou art my beloved Son; in Thee I am well pleased" (Luke 3:21–22). It is no more than suggested by the evangelists that others besides Jesus and John saw this vision and heard these words. Primarily they were meant for these two: a divine benediction on the redemptive work of the Son of Mary now openly begun; and the staggering sign that had been promised to John as he was called from the desert, "He upon whom thou shalt see the Spirit descending, and remaining upon Him, He it is that baptizeth with the Holy Ghost" (John 1:33). In that moment, John tasted the joy and terror of Joseph and Mary at Bethlehem; he knew he stood in the presence of the Son of God. His own baptism was a shadowy symbol of the reality to be given in the name of the Father, Son and Holy Ghost, not to call men to penance but to reach into their souls and undo the sins that bound them in the slavery of evil; his own work of preparation was nearly finished. He would attack what there was left of it, exultantly, watching the night of prophecy fade at the dawning of the day whose promise had lighted all the hopes of all the hearts of all the centuries. Even in the obscurity of this first light, so much of the wonders of the new day could already be dimly traced: justice, mercy, charity, penance, the unselfish strength and thoughtful understanding of one driven by a thirst for the souls of men; the Trinity, Father, Son and Holy Ghost, hinted at in the angel's message to Mary and now more clearly stated; the divinity of Mary's Son; and the obedience that is the authentic stamp on every detail of the pattern of men's salvation. John had done much more than announce the arrival of a person.

There is no account of any interchange between Jesus and John after the divine confirmation of the Messias. Silence is the only response of the humble to the presence of God; and it was not yet time, the preparation of men was not yet sufficient, for the Lord to begin His work among men. John continued his preaching and baptizing, his preparation of the ways of the Lord, seeing no more of Jesus for all of forty days. As quietly as He had come, Christ disappeared from the crowd at the Jordan. The account of the ensuing days can have come only from the lips of Christ Himself, just as the account of the beginnings of His infant life can have come only from the lips of His Mother; this one is as shatteringly human as the former was breathlessly divine.

"And Jesus being full of the Holy Ghost, returned from the Jordan, and was led by the Spirit into the desert, for the space of forty days; and was tempted by the devil" (Luke 4:1–2). "And when He had fasted forty days and forty nights, afterwards He was hungry"

(Matt. 4:2). Here was a man exposed to Satan's evil power when human nature would be at its weakest; for a lonely man, weakened by long hunger, worn with fatigue, finds it easy indeed to reach for the poisonous consolations that give so much immediate promise and move so inexorably to complete devastation. We, who have known so much of the pity of God, are not surprised, though eternally grateful, that the Son of God began His public life as man by days so patently steeped in thoughtfulness for the flickering courage of men, who would all endure the torment of temptation. These temptations of Christ were for our help, conquering our temptations by His as later He conquered our death by His own; they were for our caution, lest some degree of God's friendship give us an illusion of security and immunity from the attacks of Satan; they were for our example, that we might know how decisively to deal with suggestions to evil; they were for our hope and our trust in His compassionate understanding of our struggles and the prompt readiness of His help. By these we would know for all time that temptations are not a sign of wickedness but an invitation to it; that there can be no dallying with the devil; that it is not the sinners already enslaved who challenge Satan's power.

From Satan's point of view, the temptation of Christ was a necessity. The threat of a redeemer for men enslaved by evil had been hanging over Satan's head for many an age; he knew the prophecies, he knew John the Baptist and his preaching. The signs pointed plainly, for an angelic intelligence such as Satan's, to mounting tension of battle to the death between sin and Saviour. Satan had to know if this man were merely a man, or in reality the Saviour of men. He could know of the virginal conception by Mary, of the sinless life of Jesus;

but the veil of humanity hid from all but the eyes of faith the divinity that alone gave the infinite value necessary for men's just redemption. Satan cannot have faith, he is the recipient of no supernatural gifts from God; he could guess, could suspect, could fear this was indeed the Son of God. He set about trying to test his conjectures by a method calculated to destroy this man's bond of friendship with God if He should prove to be no more than man. It was a truly diabolic test: to uncover divine power if it were there; if it were not, to destroy the soul of a man until now sinless.

It is only by the enticement of suggestion that an enemy can attack the sovereign will of man; the suggestion must appeal, at least in appearance, to the already established affections of a man or it is stupidly ineffective. There was an unwilling compliment in the devil's use of the same plan of attack on Christ that had been so effective on Adam and Eve: nothing gross at first, nothing gravely sinful; but starting from small, even reasonable things, step by step leading up to final crescendo of evil's rejection of God. No man finds himself in the enslaving clutches of sin suddenly, surprisingly, without an undergraduate course in evil. In the case of our first parents, Satan had started with a civil-appearing question about the limitation of their choice of food, then on to the vainglory of widened knowledge ("your eyes will be opened"), to the final appeal to pride's absurd pretenses ("you shall be like God"). It is only thus that a spiritual man may be made vulnerable to evil. Christ was hungry; and perhaps he falsely believed Himself to be the Son of God. "If thou be the Son of God, command that these stones be made bread" (Matt. 4:3). Why shouldn't Christ eat, why shouldn't He show the power, if He had the power? But John had lived in these deserts without miracles, so too could Christ. Our Lord's answer gave Satan none of the desired information: "It is written, Not in bread alone doth man live; but in every word that proceedeth from the mouth of God" (Matt. 4:4). Still doubtful, Satan appealed to a weakness found even in spiritual men when he invited Christ to the vanity of ostentatious work, calling on the Scriptures themselves to give his challenge a sanctimonious air: "If Thou be the Son of God, cast Thyself down [from the pinnacle of the temple]. For it is written: He shall give His angels charge over Thee, and in their hands shall they bear Thee up lest Thou dash Thy foot against a stone" (Matt. ibid). Jesus' answer was another refusal to show divine power, and a more exasperating defeat of the devil's deeper purposes of information: "It is written again: Thou shalt not tempt the Lord thy God" (Matt. 4:6). Throwing subtlety to the winds, in a rush of hatred thick with the stupidity of anger, Satan offered the appeal of riches and the glory of the world to the contempt of God, an offer revolting to a spiritual man. There is no place here for the mocking preface "if thou be the Son of God," for this invitation is obviously in complete contradiction to the majesty of divinity. "The devil took Him up into a very high mountain, and shewed Him all the kingdoms of the world, and the glory of them. And said to Him: 'All these will I give thee if falling down, thou wilt adore me' " (Matt. 4:8–9). The open insult to God was too much to be borne; the anger of Christ flares out for the first time in the gospel story as He turns storming on the devil: "Begone Satan: for it is written, The Lord thy God shalt thou adore, and Him only shalt thou serve" (Matt. 4:10).

"Then the devil left Him; and behold angels came and

ministered to Him." St. Matthew's sculptured words of conclusion tell us something of the ordeal to human nature of this long forty days of loneliness, fatigue, hunger, and diabolic hostility. Only one other time in the life of the Saviour are we told that angels ministered to Him. That was after the agony and bloody sweat in the moonlight of the Garden of Gethsemani.

Meanwhile, the Baptist had continued his work of preparation through all these long days. Day by day the multitudes pouring to the mouth of the Jordan increased, their expectancy mounting until its tension, and the threat it carried to the position and authority of Scribes and Pharisees, could no longer be ignored by them. The delegation sent to interrogate John on the scene of his labors, instead of dampening the ardor of the people, brought it to a white heat. They crowded about to hear the questions and answers. The Baptist's voice rang with a certitude that was infectious: no, I am not the Christ; no, I am not Elias; I am the voice of one crying in the wilderness, make straight the way of the Lord. These questioners were enemies, and in the face of their hostility John did not betray the person of the Messias though Jesus, returned from the desert, could have been pointed out: "there hath stood one in the midst of you, whom you know not. The same is he that shall come after me, who is preferred before me: the latchet of whose shoe I am not worthy to loose" (John 1:26–27).

The next day after this inquisition, in the midst of the friendly crowd, "John saw Jesus coming to him, and he saith: Behold the Lamb of God, behold him who taketh away the sin of the world. This is he, of whom I said: after me there cometh a man who is preferred before me: because he was before me. And I knew him not, but that he may be made manifest in Israel, therefore am I come baptizing with water. . . . I saw the Spirit coming down, as a dove from heaven, and he remained upon him. And I knew him not; but he who sent me to baptize with water, said to me: He upon whom thou shalt see the Spirit descending, and remaining upon him, he it is that baptizeth with the Holy Ghost. And I saw, and I gave testimony, that this is the Son of God" (John 1:29–34). The testimony of the precursor leaves nothing of vagueness. Now at last the Son of Mary and of God is out of the shadows of Nazareth, identified to all the people authoritatively, and set upon His road to Calvary. Behold the man.

It was the day after this open testimony that John with two of his disciples, Andrew and John, saw Jesus walking by and again gave open testimony: "Behold the Lamb of God." This time, his testimony fell on the ears of men of Galilee, men disposed to do something about it. It was the tenth hour, about four o'clock in the afternoon, when they accosted Jesus; as happens so often in the dealings of God with men, they got much more than they had asked. It was not information as to His living quarters that He gave them, but an invitation to come with Him. They stayed with Him, that evening, and probably all through the night. They had heard the preparatory preaching of John, had heard, or had heard of, the testimony of God Himself at the baptism of Jesus, and the unmistakable identification by John; now there was to be added to all that a personal flavor of admiration and the beginnings of loyalty from the impact on heart and mind of the personality of Christ.

Andrew and John were men of the outdoors, fishermen, men who day by day wrested their living from the sea; men who sailed with danger as a shipmate, who took in their stride both the beauty and violence of nature, familiar with stars, and dawns, and sunsets. Such men are direct, uncompromising, exacting in their fundamental approval of a man; their approach to Jesus was respectful, giving Him the highest title at their command when they called Him Rabbi or master. But there was no mistaking the caution of their approach, and its clear implication that the manhood of Christ was to be brought up for judgment by these men. They would discover first and foremost what kind of a man He was. The first impressions were good. What Jesus had of inherited characteristics were Mary's made masculine, a heritage untainted, perfect, the product of divine preparation through the centuries; from Joseph He had the heritage of heavy labor challenging and nourishing strength, and the craftsman's profession with its insistent demand for self-reliant skill. Through the long hours of that first conversation, they would come under the spell of the wisdom and the prudence that are a leader's indispensable intellectual gifts; and, since virtue is the soul enlivening all a man's words and actions, they would see more than a glimpse of this man's justice, His self-controlling temperance, the courage without rashness, and the total absence of the empty defenses of pride. As men of Israel searching for the Saviour, they would look for and find in Him the reverence for God that is the guarantee of championship of men.

There was here no blinding flash of divine wisdom such as had so amazed the doctors in the Temple in this man's adolescence. John and Andrew were not amazed; they were challenged, enthralled, caught up as every man is by one who is all he himself would wish to be. Here was a man; and they would know more of Him. Friendship was sealed; companionship assured. Andrew lost no time finding his brother Simon to give him the great news: "We have found the Messias. And he brought him to Jesus. And Jesus looking upon him, said: 'Thou art Simon the son of Jona: thou shalt be called Cephas, which is interpreted Peter [the rock]' " (John 1:41–42). The initiative was all from Andrew's enthusiasm, but it met a parallel enthusiasm and quick docility from Peter. No doubt these men attached none of the profound significance, made so plain later, to the name newly bestowed on Simon by the Lord, perhaps there was enough in Peter's physical appearance and his position among his fellows to make the name as unsurprising as a particularly apt nickname. The enthusiasm of John, Andrew, and Peter at this early moment must not be confounded with the complete dedication that would be demanded of them later when they were called by Jesus to follow Him, leaving all things. Now they were not being called, rather they were being introduced, gently, persuasively, in human preparation for the call of grace that would demand so much more than human nature of itself could possibly give. For the moment, these enthusiastic friends of Christ shared the common opinion of the people: they looked for a great king whose triumph would save his people, avenge their sorrows, and overwhelm their enemies.

There was no need to dally further at the Jordan, and the next day Jesus decided to return to Galilee for it was there He Himself would make manifest His mission. Naturally, these three Galileans, drawn so close to Him in so short a time, would accompany Him. They travelled together, probably by the shortest route, following the river to the southern end of Lake Tiberias, and then by boat to its northerly shores and Bethsaida, the city of Andrew and Peter. Here Jesus found Philip and, with a simplicity stark in its contrast to the rich preparation of Andrew and John, said: "Follow me" (John 1:43). The invitation was accepted promptly; in his enthusiasm, Philip immediately sought out Nathanael, at home and at his ease, and blurted out the good news: "We have found him of whom Moses in the law, and the prophets did write, Jesus the son of Joseph of Nazareth" (John 1:45). Nathanael (the Bartholomew of Matthew, Mark and Luke), a man of Cana, indulged the compatriot's easy contempt for a neighboring town: "Can anything of good come from Nazareth?", only to receive the perfect answer from Philip: "Come and see" (John 1:46). Nathanael remained the open-minded investigator even in the face of Jesus' flattering greeting of him as an Israelite without guile. His complete capitulation at Christ's words, "when thou wast under the fig tree, I saw thee," tells us plainly that more was said in these words than could be understood by any but Christ and Nathanael himself. Something had happened in the man's soul under the fig tree, and the evidence that this intimately personal experience was known by Christ scattered all his doubt: "Rabbi, thou art the Son of God, thou art the king of Israel" (John 1:49). Neither Philip nor Nathanael saw Christ as more than the envoy of God; that was enough for the moment. There would be more to see, more to hear, enough indeed to win a man's faith in the divinity of Jesus Himself; and that before very long.

The wedding feast at Cana was to furnish the occasion for the first manifestation of Our Lord's divine power before these newly-won friends. That feast was on the third day after the arrival of the pilgrims at Bethsaida. Probably Philip had made the short trip to Cana to enlist Nathanael, and had brought the latter back to see Jesus for himself. From him they would know of the feast, and of Jesus having been invited. St. John records the previous presence of Mary in the East's most respectful address, stressing the woman's high honor of motherhood; "the mother of Jesus was there." The whole company made their way to the little town to add to the gaiety of an occasion that always and everywhere has been soundly seen as a reason for rejoicing. In this case, there was much more involved than the social gesture of friendship; by his approving presence, Jesus gave a divine approval to the institution of marriage, more, He gave it a divine consecration to make of it a channel of grace, an instrument of divine life for the souls of bride and groom, forever condemning the evil minds who would see in marriage something bestially beneath the dignity of man, and the equally evil minds that would see man as too bestial to live up to the solemn obligations of the sacrament. Neither the "pure" ones who desecrate the very notion of home, nor the perpetual adolescents whose supreme law is convenience and pleasure, can look for support to the Son of Mary.

In a country of vineyards like Galilee, this was a time for wine and the rejoicing of the heart of man which is the boon of its moderate use. These were humble people in Cana, and the wine had been hoarded for many a day in preparation for this happy day, yet the wine was running short; to have poverty so underlined and emphasized would be a tragedy of embarrassment for the fierce pride of the poor. Perhaps Mary had half expected just this when she saw the crowd arrive with her Son; certainly her motherly alertness detected the situation before anyone else's attention was attracted to it. In a rush of pity, with full knowledge of this divine person who was her Son, she turned to Him quietly and said simply; "They have no wine." So simply! He had worked no miracles for her, not even in the face of mortal danger, of grinding poverty, of death's bitter loss. He was her God, and she adored Him. She was His mother, and He loved her. Gently, delicately, confidently she asked that He use that divine power for love of her in favor of these poor friends, that their joy be not turned into shamed sorrow.

Considering only the Greek, the language in which the words were written down, the answer of Jesus reads thus: "Woman, what is that to thee and to Me? My hour is not yet come." Read thus, it is surely misunderstood. There is, of course, no severity or disrespect in the address "Woman"; it is a respectful, if somewhat solemn, form of address in the Greek as well as in the Hebrew. For the rest of that first sentence, we must look to the language in which Christ spoke, the Aramaic, and then recognize that His words were: "Woman, never mind"; i.e., it is not for us to intervene here. Without disrespect, without brusqueness, the words are still a refusal; and for the reason stated: He had not intended to appear so before men until John the Baptist had finished his mission. Mary, who all her life had asked so little and nothing for herself, had love's privilege of seeing beyond words; she knew, for all the previous plans, that she had not been refused. As many another woman after her has done, she went on as if the refusal had never been spoken, and said to the waiters: "Whatsoever He shall say to you, do ye." What was to be done, how it was to be done, was none of her affair; but that the necessary thing would be done was her certitude. The obedient, if puzzled, waiters filled six huge stone vessels with water at Jesus's direction; still under His orders, from the water-filled vessels, they drew off the best wine of the feast. It was all done so smoothly and quietly as to attract no one's attention; but it is difficult indeed to hide a miracle, and there was the good wine where none had been before. The bride-groom would be eager in his testimony of the extravagance of God; his very poverty would now be not an embarrassment but an occasion of God's tenderness.

The impression of this first miracle of Jesus upon His disciples was profound; they believed in Him, believed that the power of God was in Him. They had none of the modern sophisticate's difficulty with miracles; it seemed to them, as it always does to the uncluttered mind, not at all contradictory for the Author of nature to do nature's work without the bother of nature's instrumentality, for surely His power was not limited by the powers He loaned to natural things. Nor was there any of the obsession of magnificence to cloud their vision. There was no apologetic explanation required for the omnipotence of God busying itself to ward off embarrassment from some country folk at their marriage feast; rather, the circumstances were confirmatory of the miracle, for it is only God who always has power to expend on little ones and little things, only God who is in a position to know how small all human things are, yet how big to the human heart the littlest of them can be.

After the wedding feast, the evangelists tell us no more of the movements of Jesus until about a month later, when the little company met at Capharnaum to set out together for Jerusalem and the first feast of the Pasch in the public life of Our Lord. It is probable that Jesus went back to Nazareth with Mary, while the others went back to their daily work of fishing on the Lake of Tiberias, agreeing to meet at Capharnaum for the pilgrimage. These early disciples were not yet firmly fixed in Jesus' company, they had not as yet been called to complete dedication to the apostolate; this way, they had a month to ponder over the wonders, from the words of John to the miracle at Cana, that pointed so squarely to the Messiahship of the Carpenter of Nazareth, time to remember, and to miss, the charm, the wisdom, the power and thc goodness of Mary's Son. When they came together again, they would be yet more ready for the faith that would open their eyes to the divine person to whom they were already so drawn.

When this short stay at home was over, "He went down to Capharnaum, He and His mother, and His brethren, and His disciples; and they remained there not many days" (John 2:12). This was a group assembled for the pilgrim's trip, not for the apostle's preparation. These "brethren," cousins of Jesus, would be among the last to surrender disbelief.

Arriving at Jerusalem "at the pasch, upon the festival day, many believed in His name, seeing His signs which He did" (John 2:23). We have been left a full account of one of those signs, and some fragmentary notes of a night-long talk with a man struggling from doubts to faith: the expulsion of the money-changers from the temple and the discussion with Nicodemus, both charged with the mystery inseparable from God's dealings with men.

The outer courts of the Temple on the occasion of the pasch were a bedlam of haggling avarice. The bleating and bellowing of animals gave a still shriller tone to the shouting voices of angry men. Some confusion was unavoidable here, since the Law demanded the sacrifices of animals and the temple tax in Jewish money. The great crowds of expatriated Jews, returning home for the feast, would have neither the animals nor the currency and would have to obtain both on the spot. The disgraceful disorder that Jesus found at this first pasch was greed's contribution to the feast. Acting so quickly that He left his disciples as gaping spectators, He made "a scourge of little cords, (and) He drove them all out of the temple, the sheep also and the oxen, and the money of changers He poured out, and the tables He overthrew. And to them that sold doves He said: Take these things hence, and make not the house of my Father a house of traffic" (John 2:15–16).

His courage, strength, and burning indignation hardly account for the complete success of His attack on greed. It remains mysterious that, His divinity as yet unknown by the crowds, His action was not challenged until it had been completed. It was only then that the authorities, those Jews whose jealous hostility had already been aroused by the Baptist, confronted Him: " 'What sign dost thou show unto us, seeing thou dost these things?' Jesus answered, and said to them: 'Destroy this temple, and in three days I will raise it up.' The Jews then said: 'Six and forty years was this temple in building; and wilt thou raise it up in three days?' But He spoke of the temple of His body" (John 2:18–21). The sign He offered was prophetic, and only the future would confirm it; nevertheless, He was not further molested in spite of the havoc He had wrought. Though their consciences would show them the justice of His action, the Jews would hold His words for later use, bringing them forth garbled as evidence that He was worthy of execution. On His side, Jesus, from these first days, held out His own resurrection from the dead as the ultimate confirmation of His words and acts. Violence came easily to men of Galilee, yet the disciples had been so startled that it was all over before they lifted a hand. They were entitled to a kind of stupefaction, for they were seeing more than the mind of a man can take in quickly; to the witness of God and the Baptist, the miraculous power of Cana for their pondering, there was now added a sweeping authority uncompromising to irreligion and greed, a wrath devastating in its effect, yet divinely tempered to the weakness of men and their frail possessions in order to correct rather than destroy.

Among those in Jerusalem who saw the signs that Jesus did was Nicodemus, one of the class with the most religious authority in Israel, the Pharisees. He was a man of good will, and the works of Jesus, coming on the heels of the preaching of the Baptist, disquieted him. If Jesus spoke the truth, He should be heard most fully; at any rate, in view of the signs He did, He surely deserved a hearing. Yet, it was a dangerous business for a man of Nicodemus' position to appear to favor in the least this man who had so angered the religious leaders by His zealous cleansing of the Temple. It was then stealthily, at night, that Nicodemus approached Jesus, at the same time giving expression to the sincerity that brought him there at all: "Rabbi, we know that thou art come a teacher from God; for no man can do these signs which thou dost, unless God be with him" (John 3:2). He came honestly, if cautiously, in search of truth, humbly as a student anxious to learn, though he was a Master in Israel; the night stretched before these two, the divine master and the sincere student, and before it was over Nicodemus would have seen the graciousness of God.

Quite aside from the patient hours given by Christ in answer to this sincerity, there is a peculiarly appealing intellectual delicacy that shows clearly even in the brief résumé we have of this long conversation. Here Our Lord puts aside the almost maternal restraint that marks all His teaching in Galilee; the sublime truths are given to Nicodemus, not morsel by morsel but in a torrent of abundance. There is an immediate challenge in the paradox of a man having to be born again to see the kingdom of God; Nicodemus, visualizing the impossibility of a physical rebirth, does not deny the paradox but asks its explanation. The answer lies in the baptism that John had foretold, the baptism by water and the Holy Ghost that Jesus is bringing to men. Here Nicodemus should begin to understand, for this word came first from the last of the prophets of the Old Law and the words were still echoing from all the hills of Judaea. At his puzzlement, Jesus gives notice of the even more sublime truths that await his believing: faith in Jesus as the Son of God, in His divine nature and person; the scandal of His death on the cross that those who believe might be saved; the generosity of God and the limitlessness of His love that would not spare His only-begotten Son, the Son sent among men, not to judge them but to save them. Jesus draws on the breaking dawn for the figures that will express with terrifying clarity the individual responsibility of each man: "And this is the judgment: because the light is come into the world, and men loved darkness rather than the light; for their works were evil. For every one that doth evil hateth the light, and cometh not to the light, that his works may not be reproved. But he that doth truth, cometh to the light, that his works may be made manifest, because they are done in God" (John 3:19–21).

After these paschal days in Jerusalem, Jesus and His disciples went down to the Jordan, not far from where John was baptizing, and stayed there some days during which the disciples of Jesus also baptized the people. This short stay was the occasion of a final testimony from the Baptist, and still one more revelation of the magnificent heart of the precursor. John's disciples complained to him that the little band of Jesus was baptizing too and that all men were flocking to them. John knew that his own work was nearly but not quite finished, and so the baptism given by Jesus' disciples was, like his own, still a preparatory thing rather than the rebirth by the Holy Spirit that was so soon to come. He gently rebuked his disciples in words that were at the same time an exultant joy in the growing fullness of the Messias. "A man cannot receive anything, unless it be given him from heaven. You yourselves do bear me witness, that I said, I am not Christ, but that I am sent before Him. He that hath the bride is the bridegroom: but the friend of the bridegroom who standeth and heareth him, rejoiceth with joy because of the bridegroom's voice. This my joy therefore is fulfilled. He must increase, but I must decrease" (John 3:27–30). The dimness of dawn was nearly done; it was time for the full light of the sun.

6

HIGH NOON IN THE NIGHT

JOHN had begun his preaching of penance in the fall; it was ended with violent abruptness the following summer. Precisely at the time that the two groups of disciples were so close to one another and baptizing, the agents of Herod Antipas, ruler of Galilee and Perea, swooped down on John to rush him off to imprisonment and ultimate martyrdom. John was mercy itself to the lowly ones who came to him for help. He could not be silent about a crime which, because it was the crime of a prince, stood out as a guiding star to viciousness for all the people. There was no answer to John's condemnation of the incestuous union of Herod with his brother's wife, no answer but the one it got: the open confession inherent in the brutal silencing of the voice of the last of the prophets.

Though the echoes of that voice would continue to ring from the hills, the imprisonment of John came as a happy coincidence to the rulers of the Jews who had become so uneasy at his preaching. It solved a part of a problem, but only a part; for since the tumult in the temple, Jesus had loomed as more of a threat to their position than John had been. Jesus was still free, He had incurred no enmity on the part of Herod; but Herod had shown that there was a decisive way to deal with these trouble makers. It was not yet time for Jesus to expose Himself to the plot of the Scribes and Pharisees; besides, now that the precursor's work had come to an end, it was time to begin in full earnest the labors in whose preparation John had been sent. At the word of John's imprisonment, Our Lord and His handful of disciples started back to Galilee and the ministry of men's salvation.

With the rulers of the Jews in their present mood it was no time to return to Jerusalem and from there take the normal pilgrim's road through Samaria; yet neither did they take the direct road north along the Jordan, though their feet were already upon it. Instead, they struck out northeast and joined the Jerusalem-Galilee road at Jacob's well, near the Samaritan town of Sichar. Whatever the reason for the choice, one woman is eternally grateful that on that particular summer day, while the disciples went into town to get provisions, Jesus sat thus on the well: tired, hot, dusty, thirsty both for water and for souls. This Samaritan woman, coming from the waterless town to the well, was undismayed at the sight of the solitary stranger there. Her succession of consorts had long since passed beyond pretensions to respectability and, following the immemorial pattern, she had donned an armor of brazenness as a feeble defense of the heart against the thrusts of universal scorn; undaunted, she came on to the well.

As St. John tells the story of that conversation between the social outcast and the Saviour, it has tones familiar to every man: the mysteriously patient wooing of a soul by God. Christ endured the needless raillery of her answer to His simple request for a drink of water; pursued her gently, delicately, persistently through her amusement at His having a gift of water to give and her open mockery of one making Himself greater than Jacob. When the divine stroke had split the armor open, and she stood embarrassed, confused, dismayed that this stranger should know what no stranger could know of her, He did not press the embarrassment beyond all bearing; rather He patiently followed her on her panicky rush to turn attention from herself by plunging into the religious dispute that made such enemies of Jews and Samaritans. Mistaking His patience for the success of her stratagem, she was ready to dismiss the whole discussion and slip back into her defenses when she was struck down by the mercy of God: "I know that the Messias cometh (who is called Christ); therefore, when He is come, He will tell us all things. Jesus saith to her: I am He, Who am speaking with thee" (John 4:25–26). There was more here than the words that were spoken. Looking into His eyes, she knew He spoke the truth. But there was more than that. The eyes that had pierced her armor to see her remorse, her courage, the betrayed trusts, the abused generosity, and even the shreds of innocence, told her plainly that the gift of God's mercy was in her hands; it was not consternation, not despair, not fright that sent her flying back to the town at the moment of the arrival of the disciples, leaving the water pitcher behind her. It was eagerness, eagerness to tell others, to shout from the housetops the news that was so good she would not hesitate to make what amounted to an open confession to convince men that it was indeed true. All the brazenness was gone now, and humility puts its authentic stamp on every one of her words to her fellow citizens: "Come and see a man who has told me all things whatsoever I have done. Is not He the Christ?"

There is high tribute to Christ recorded in the simple

words: "They (the disciples) wondered that He talked with the woman. Yet no man said: What seekest thou? Or: Why talkest thou with her?" It was unheard of that a man publicly talk to such a woman; but here was a man who had won their respect, their affection, and a degree of their trust beyond anything they themselves had as yet realized. In such circumstances, what cannot be understood is not grounds for suspicion but for renewed faith. Then, too, the woman the disciples saw was a different person from the one who had come to Christ, and a miracle of grace before their very eyes does not leave men unshaken. It was important that the disciples, here at the very beginning, see recovered innocence, see the scars of vice lose their ugliness, see the grim winter of sin banished in an instant by the vigorous vitality of an unending spring; it was good for them to see the hope and joy and unutterable happiness of this woman who had come for water and received grace. For they must know the meat that nourishes the apostle, they must know the persistent divine will to save men, they must see the harvest of souls waiting to be reaped, a harvest ready now as the golden fields that looked so white under the glaring sun.

"Now of that city many of the Samaritans believed in Him, for the word of the woman giving testimony . . . so when the Samaritans were come to Him, they desired that He would tarry there . . . and many more believed in Him because of His own word. And they said to the woman: We now believe, not for thy saying: for we ourselves have heard Him, and know that this is indeed the Saviour of the world" (John 4:39, 40, 41–42).

"Now after two days, He departed thence, and went into Galilee" (John 4:43). On the way north, there was time to ponder this episode of the Samaritans. Jesus had stopped to give divine gifts to a sinner scorned of men, and had tarried to minister to the enemies of His race; His words to the disciples had stressed both the terrible urgency and the unconditioned universality of the mission on which He, and they, were about to embark—a harvest of souls too ripe to suffer delay by the reapers. They would not easily forget the response of God to the welcome of men. Now Galilee lay ahead and the beginning of that campaign for souls; it was there that the light was first to cast its full brilliance upon men, as Isaias had foretold: "Land of Zabulon, and land of Nephthalim, the way of the sea beyond the Jordan, Galilee of the Gentiles! The people that sat in darkness hath seen great light, and on them that sat in the region of the shadow of death, light is sprung up" (Isai. 9:1–2; Matt. 4:15–16).

The little band came to Cana in Galilee, the privileged town which had witnessed the first miracle of Christ and now saw that divine power strike out across the miles to cure the son of the court official who had climbed the hills of Nazareth searching in desperation for Jesus. The distraught father was almost mannerless in his impatient demands that Jesus come down to his son; both his limited faith, balking at distance, and his impatience were sympathetically understood by Jesus who said to him: "Go thy way; thy son liveth" (John 4:50). The man believed, believed so strongly that he did not hurry back to verify the miracle; it was only the next day, as he made his way home, that his servants came with the news. Then "himself believed, and his whole house." These flashes of divine lightning preceding the storm of divine power struck in oddly different places: a marriage feast of the poor, the traders in the Temple, the scholar in the dead of night, the brazen

Samaritan woman, and now the Jewish boy of a courtly family. Seen together, as the disciples could hardly help seeing them, they already told much of the divine Son of Mary; the preparation of the disciples for their divine vocation was almost complete.

The shock at the confrontation of divine power, the essence of a miracle, sent a tremor through the countryside. ". . . and the fame of Him went out through the whole country. And He taught in their synagogues, and was magnified by all" (Luke 4:14). Jesus began His teaching in Nazareth, the town of Mary and Joseph. Naturally, His teaching began in the synagogue which was, after all, primarily a school of the Law since worship was restricted to the Temple in Jerusalem. There was nothing unusual in His reading a passage from the Scriptures and expounding it; it was common practice for one of the congregation, or a passing guest, to be called on for this task. His text and its application were far from ordinary. " 'The Spirit of the Lord is upon me. Wherefore he hath anointed me to preach the gospel to the poor, he hath sent me to heal the contrite of heart, to preach deliverance to the captives, and sight to the blind, to preach the acceptable year of the Lord, and the day of reward.' And when He had folded the book, He restored it to the minister, and sat down. And the eyes of all in the synagogue were fixed on Him. And He began to say to them: This day is fulfilled this scripture in your ears. And all gave testimony to Him: and they wondered at the words of grace that proceeded from His mouth, and they said: Is not this the son of Joseph?" (Luke 4:18–22). Later on He would not be so graciously listened to and admired in Nazareth, but at this opening of His ministry it was not yet time for persecution. Neither was Nazareth the place to catch the eyes, the minds, and the hearts of men. After this gracious gesture, He left Nazareth for good to take up His residence, if He could ever again be said to have a residence, in the thriving city of Capharnaum.

The people of Capharnaum, like those of Galilee, were no such hair-splitting legalists as their brethren of Judaea and Jerusalem. They accepted the burden of the Law and the much heavier burden of the interpretations that extended the Law to every detail of a man's whole life; nor did they question the equalizing of these interpretations with the Law itself. Yet, as simple people so often do, they penetrated to the heart of Christ's teaching at His first appearance in the synagogue at Capharnaum; they saw at once the issue by which are divided those who follow Christ and those who crucify Him. "And they were astonished at His doctrine. For He was teaching them as one having authority, and not as the scribes" (Mark 1:22). He taught with authority; not calling for support, not herding all things within the narrow fences of the Law, not appealing to higher sanctions; but with *His own authority*. He was God, and He taught as God teaches. Men accept His divinity or forever exclude Him from their lives.

This was a fast-moving day in the history of Capharnaum. The city was submerged in a flood of divine truth confirmed by divine power. While they were still in the synagogue, the devil cried out in the voice of a man he had possessed: "Let us alone, what have we to do with thee, Jesus of Nazareth? Art thou come to destroy us? I know thee who thou art, the holy one of God" (Luke 4:34). A word from Jesus and the devil was vanquished: "Hold thy peace and go out of him. And when the devil had thrown him into the midst, he went out of him, and hurt him not at all. And there came fear upon

all, and they talked among themselves saying; What word is this, for with authority and power He commandeth the unclean spirits, and they go out? And the fame of Him was published into every place in the country" (Luke 4:35–37). From the synagogue, Jesus with James and John, Peter and Andrew, went to Peter's house; there at a touch of the hand of Jesus, Peter's mother-in-law rose from her sick bed, cured of her fever in an instant, and ministered to them. As soon as the sun had set and the sabbath restrictions on movement were lifted, "all the city was gathered together at the door" (Mark 1:33). "They brought to Him many that were possessed with devils: and He cast out the spirits with His word: and all that were sick He healed" (Matt. 8:16).

How far into the night that confirmation of authoritative teaching by the ministry of mercy extended, we do not know; but it was early in the morning, before daybreak, that Jesus slipped out of the house for solitude and prayer, for He was man as well as God, with all of a man's spiritual needs. It was the impulsive Peter, eager to take up the triumph of yesterday, who sought Him out with the words: "All seek Thee." But it was not to one city alone that Christ had come; there were other towns and cities to be told unmistakably that the kingdom of God had come. To them Jesus went, all through Galilee preaching in their synagogues and confirming His words with a steady flow of miracles which freed the possessed from the domination of the devil and restored health to the sick whatever their maladies. Divine authority, divine truth, and divine power fell on the hills and valleys of Galilee like a steady rain on a parched land; men everywhere drank of that life-giving water and came alive with hope.

Peter's enthusiasm at Capharnaum was still far from the divine fire that consumes all the days of an apostle. Indeed, it is quite possible that Jesus was unaccompanied on much of His travels through Galilee, teaching and healing; for the few disciples He had been so gently preparing had returned to the routine of daily labors that filled their lives before they had met the Son of Mary. Meanwhile the tide of His teaching had risen far above the confining walls of the synagogue. So it was that on one day Jesus, surrounded by crowds on the shore of the Lake of Galilee, was giving them the priceless gift of the word of God when He noticed two fishing ships pulling into the shore after a night's work on the lake. They were the ships of Peter and Andrew, and of James and John, the sons of Zebedee; yet these friends of His did not rush to join the crowd about Jesus but went on to the routine conclusion of their work by washing their nets. Jesus boarded the ship of Peter and asked him to pull out a little, and from there the Lord continued the instruction of the people crowding the shore. When he had finished, and as though in divine payment for so slight a service, He told the fishermen to put out to sea again and let down their nets. Peter was elaborately patient. Though it was evident to any man that they had had no success through all the hours of the night, he was willing, if Christ insisted, to do as he was told. The result was a miraculous draught of fishes that so swamped Peter and Andrew as to make it necessary to call on their partners for help. It did much more than that. In that moment, the last traces of hesitation, caution, or reluctance disappeared from the hearts of the fishermen; the divine power exercised for the first time directly in their favor sent them to their knees in humble adoration that found its heartfelt expression in the words of Peter: "Depart from me, O Lord, for I am a sinful man."

They were at last ready. "And Jesus said to them: Come after Me, and I will make you to become fishers of men. And immediately leaving their nets, they followed Him" (Mark 1:17). Behind them as they faced forward with Christ there were ranged parents, a wife, ships and nets, all that had gone into the lives they had lived up to this moment; they left everything, even the miraculous draught of fishes! There would be no turning back. No rewards had been dangled before their eyes, no promises made, no predictions beyond the good that would come to the men and women to whom they would be sent. This divine call is answered, not for what can be had from the answering, but for what can be given in gratitude for the call; it is love's answer to a challenging love, the only possible answer, the answer of complete dedication, utter surrender.

From the many miracles that Jesus had done in confirmation of His tireless teaching, the Evangelists now select one for treatment in detail. It comes, as a fitting climax of wonder, gentleness, and law-abiding respect, to close this period of unchallenged proclamation of the kingdom of God. A man full of leprosy, in flagrant disobedience of the Law's commands, came into the city, entered the house where Jesus was staying and threw himself on his knees before Our Lord. The horror of the disease and the dread of its mysterious contagion had made for a ruthless defense against it by the society of that time: the leper was as one dead, he must wear a distinctive garment so as to be easily recognized, live apart from the habitations of all men, and even give warning of his condition to anyone thoughtlessly approaching him. His cry of "Unclean" brought no mercy from others, and no comfort to himself as his body rotted away. This leper, full of the disease, was driven by his misery and his faith to the feet of Jesus; he had no time to lose in making his supplication, for discovery would mean an instant stoning from the city. Indeed, he lost no time; to Jesus, from his knees, he said simply: "If Thou wilt, Thou canst make me clean." The answer was no less quick: "I will. Be thou made clean" (Mark 1:40–41). Before the astounded eyes of the disciples, as He spoke the words, reaching out He touched the leper. In that instant the man was cured, every inch of his body delivered from the slow corruption of leprosy. "And He charged him that he should tell no man, but 'Go, show thyself to the priest, and offer for thy cleansing according as Moses commanded, for a testimony to them' " (Luke 5:14).

There was, of course, no hiding of such a miracle, no disguising the healthy cleanliness of a skin that a moment before had been leprous. But it was important that the cured man should not, in his exuberance, forget the obligations he was under by the Law. Jesus here, in the early days of His ministry, was being particularly careful to give men time to correct their erroneous notions of the Messias as a temporal prince sweeping all enemies before him and exacting full vengeance on the Romans. Given time, His authority, the truth He spoke, the power He exercised should let men see that His kingdom was not of this earth, that the state of a man's soul was of more importance than the state of the empire, the glory of God's reign in a man's heart much more to the point than the glory of Israel. So there is no challenge to the Law which He had come to fulfil and replace, His Messiahship is deliberately toned down; as far as His essential mission allows it, He is not focusing attention on Himself in the crowded marts of men. After this miracle of the leper, He went out into the desert places and prayed as He had done before and was to do again; but now He stayed in those desert places, avoiding the great cities, and yet, as St. Mark points out, the people came flocking out to Him even there.

Eventually in all its length and breadth Galilee had heard His word, seen His signs, marvelled at His authority. He moved throughout this period on a trail of glory; the light of the truth stunning men's minds with its brightness, the divine authority gripping men's hearts with a healthy fear that is the beginning of wisdom, the miracles removing all limits to the scope of men's hopes. By this time, Jesus could no longer enter openly into a city or show Himself on the streets without being thronged by the enthusiastic, hope-thirsty crowds. These were glorious days in Galilee; but they were now at an end.

At the close of this period of simple, joyous welcome, we find Jesus slipping quietly into Capharnaum to avoid the crowds; but the refuge He found in the house there was only a momentary one. Privacy was hardly expected, certainly not respected, in the Orient of those days, as in ours. He was soon discovered, not only by the people to whom He was the fulfilment of hope, but also by the perverse men to whom He was fast becoming a threat. The house soon filled and overflowed into the street; up front, as though in places of honor, the scribes and Pharisees seated themselves but not in the same frame of mind as the men who crowded every inch of space behind them. This was the first time, since that violent scene in the Temple, that the opposition of men to the gifts of God was made a challenge to be met flatly and openly. As Jesus talked, the flimsy roof over His head was parted and a man sick of the palsy, helpless on his mat or bed, was lowered to the floor before Jesus. No word was spoken, either by the man himself or by the friends who, unable to push their way through the crowd, had taken this drastic means to come to Christ. Certainly the gesture itself was a sufficient protestation of faith; the merciful eyes of the Son of God read the heart of the sick man and His lips gave immediate response to the needs and desires He saw there: "Son, thy sins are forgiven thee" (Mark 2:5). "And there were some of the scribes sitting there, and thinking in their hearts: Why doth this man speak thus? He blasphemeth. Who can forgive sins but God only?" (Mark 2:5–6).

These men got the point reached so much earlier by the simple ones who first listened to Him in Capharnaum: He spoke with authority. He was not calling upon God's mercy for the forgiveness of this man's sins; He was, by His own authority, doing what only God can do—directly forgiving the sins. The conclusion was perfectly clear: either this man is God or He is a blasphemer and an impostor. The scribes and Pharisees were much too cautious to make open protest; but Jesus, reading their hearts as He had read the sick man's, paraded the challenge before the assembled multitude and met it squarely. "That you may know that the Son of man hath power on earth to forgive sins, (He saith to the sick of the palsy): I say to thee: Arise, take up thy bed, and go into thy house. And immediately he arose; and taking up his bed, went his way in the sight of all; so that all wondered and glorified God, saying: We never saw the like" (Mark 2:10–12). The man who had been touched body and soul by the finger of God had no difficulty getting out of the house; the crowds melted before him. But not all glorified God. The hostile leaders were impressed neither by the searching of their hearts by Christ nor by the miracle in explicit confirmation of divine authority over the souls of men. This was the beginning, and the story would remain the same to the end: it was not for evil alleged against the Son of Mary but for the good He did to men that these envious ones would hound His footsteps.

These conflicts with the leaders of the Jews would not be of Jesus' seeking, yet there would be no escape from them. To avoid further turmoil and to escape from the crowds for the moment, Jesus left Capharnaum; but the crowds followed Him. Yielding to their importunities, He taught them more of the truths for which they so hungered. As He went along the shore of the Lake of Galilee, He came to a tax-gatherer's booth and there saw Matthew, the publican, at his work. The contempt in which this profession was held was so profound that Luke and Mark, recording the event, hide the identity of the publican under his Jewish name of Levi; it was only the humility of the man himself, writing later as Matthew the apostle and evangelist, that made it clear that this Levi was indeed Matthew. As Jesus passed He pronounced two momentous words: Follow me. Immediately, leaving everything behind him for all time, Matthew took up the apostle's tracing of the footsteps of the Master. In these unadorned words of Christ, there is the same divine power that cured the leper and forgave the sins of the man with palsy; for these words were a divine call signalling the flood of supernatural help that makes it possible for men of all ages to do the impossible, leaving all things and following Him.

No further words were exchanged; the matter was settled. To the eternal puzzlement of the men of the world, the eager thanks were not on God's side for so unconditional an answer from man but on man's side for the opportunity to respond. So it has always been. Matthew, a silent man, could find no words for his thanks, but thanks there had to be; in such circumstances, the best a man can do is to throw open his house in welcome, hoping that thus it will be made plain how wide open are the doors of his heart. Matthew prepared a dinner for his newly found Master; the other guests would be the disciples of Christ and the company in which alone Matthew was at home—a gathering of publicans and sinners. The curious could follow the course of the meal as onlookers, indeed it was almost their right in the East's easy disregard of privacy. The Pharisees were there, not in curiosity but in pursuit of their constant program of sly detection. They were scandalized. These guests with whom Jesus was so much at home were careless of the Law, undoubtedly guilty of legal impurities, and quite possibly men of corrupt lives; any slightest contact with them was beneath the legalism and ostentatious piety of the Pharisees. Yet, in their slyness, it was not Jesus they challenged, but some of His disciples. Their challenge was overheard, and the answer cut to the heart of their own disregard of the souls of men. "Why doth your Master eat and drink with publicans and sinners? Jesus hearing this, saith to them: They that are well have no need of a physician, but they that are sick. For I came not to call the just, but sinners" (Mark 2:16–17).

The Pharisees, themselves professed physicians of the people, would take none of the physician's risk of contagion in ministering to the spiritually sick; and by that fact abandoned rightful title to their position as leaders of the people. Here was one who had come precisely to do the work of the physician of souls; those who accepted His invitation and did indeed follow Him must take all the risks to save sinners. To a thinking Pharisee the words of Christ offered material for serious pondering. "I came not to call the just but sinners"; whence had He come, where had He been and for how long? Who was He? The answers were solutions to all the difficulties they had raised or would raise against Him: for He was the eternal son of God, coming to the womb of the virgin to take on human nature, coming to dwell amongst men that their sins might be forgiven them.

These two continue throughout the remaining days of Our Lord's life—the depth of His answers, and the persistent opposition of the scribes and Pharisees; both become more clear and open as the conflict grows sharper. The first opposition of the enemies of Christ was hidden in their hearts, revealed only by the Lord's divine insight into the souls of men; more boldly the next time, they complained to His disciples. On one day, not long after the call of Matthew, they spoke up to Christ Himself: "They come and say to Him: why do the disciples of John and of the Pharisees fast; but thy disciples do not fast?" There was no infringement of the Law at issue here; the question was rather aimed at discrediting Christ and His little band in the eyes of the people. Only the Day of Atonement was a fast of obligation for all the people; many other days of fast and mourning had been set aside for observance by the tradition that heaped burdens on the people without authority for those burdens. The explicitly pious, such as the Pharisees and some of the zealots of John's following, could compare themselves favorably with Jesus and His disciples in the observance of these days; the implicit conclusion being that Christ and His followers were not pious men.

Our Lord's answer goes far beyond the question.

These are not days of mourning but of rejoicing for His friends who still have Him, the bridegroom, with them. "But the days will come when the bridegroom shall be taken away from them; and then they shall fast in those days" (Mark 2:20). To a people used to savoring each morsel of a figure of speech, the veiled reference to Christ's death would not be missed though it would hardly as yet be understood; it is not the bridegroom who is taken away from his friends after the marriage feast, but his friends who take themselves off and leave the bridegroom to his bride. Here there is a note of violence introduced; a disruption of the marriage feast that is a reason for mourning for all the centuries of men. Something new has been introduced into the world to put an end for all time to the periods of mourning of the old Law. "No man seweth a piece of raw cloth to an old garment"; as some of John's disciples attempted to do, engrafting the new principle of penance on the old garment of Pharisaism; inevitably the shrinking of the new will tear the old. "No man putteth new wine into old bottles: otherwise the wine will burst the bottles, and both the wine will be spilled, and the bottles will be lost. But new wine must be put into new bottles" (Mark 2:22). The old leathern bottles, worn thin by time, cannot stand the strong, active fermentation of the new. It is not a reform of the Law, nor an addition to it; but a fulfilment, a new Law, that is now brought to men by the Son of God Himself. The point plainly made is that to receive a new teaching, men must be made new, detached from the observances created by a tradition without real authority. This contract between the new and the old brought nothing of comfort to the Pharisees who gave a false antiquity to the newest innovation to bolster it with the sanctions of the Law. The answer of Christ served only to increase their uneasiness and sharpen their sly opposition. The issue was poised more clearly with each conflict: it was less and less a question of whether He spoke the truth, and more and more a worry lest their position of authority be undermined.

One Sabbath day in early June, Jesus and His disciples were walking down a road through the fields of grain just ripening for the harvest, which is so much later here in upper Galilee than in the low country of Samaria. Absent-mindedly, or in positive hunger, the disciples plucked handfuls of grain and munched on them as they strolled along. The ever present Pharisees were quick to pounce, confronting Jesus Himself with the accusation of violation of the Law: "Behold thy disciples do that which is not lawful to do on the Sabbath days" (Matt. 12:2). The accusation did not turn on the journey which was under way, for they themselves were in the company; nor was it a question of property rights in the face of the universal and ancient customs of the East which explicitly permitted the passing wayfarer nourishment. Harvesting the grain on the Sabbath was formally forbidden in the Law; and this, in the interpretation of the Pharisees, was harvesting. That His disciples violated both the spirit and the practices of the Pharisees Jesus would admit cheerfully; but never in all of His life would He tolerate the accusation of disobedience to the Law. It was not He who violated the Law, but the Pharisees who had falsified that Law against all the benevolent intentions of the divine legislator. Here, in this case, He did not descend to casuistic details of the prohibitions of the Sabbath, but plunged immediately to the fundamental principle which in one stroke destroyed all the rabbinical appendices that had made the Sabbath impossible of observation. There is no special benefit to God from men's observation of the Sabbath; He did not create men to guard the Sabbath; "the Sabbath was made for man, not man for the Sabbath" (Mark 2:27). Positive laws do not oblige to man's detriment; they are made in his interest. Under the pressure of necessity, they yield to the benefit of man. The priests in the temple break the Sabbath in their functions and are not held guilty; "but I tell you that there is here a greater than the Temple" (Matt. 12:6). "For the Son of man is Lord even of the Sabbath" (Matt. 12:8). Greater than the Temple, Lord even of the Sabbath; with all that had gone before these words, only a cultivated blindness on the part of the Pharisees could miss the unveiling of the Messias who had come to save men, not merely to vindicate a nation. The divine kindness, at each challenge, gave so much more than had been asked; and at each gift of truth, the perverse ones retreated deeper into their darkness lest the light of the truth threaten what they cherished so.

The exasperated anger and seething envy of the Pharisees reached volcanic proportions in a synagogue at Capharnaum; the furious eruption there fixed the hearts and minds of the Pharisees against Christ as firmly as though they had been submerged in a flood of hot lava. A victim of paralysis had come to the synagogue on a Sabbath hoping to find a cure for his withered right hand in the power of Jesus. Knowing this, the Pharisees, athirst for revenge against Jesus for the sharp blade of truth He had wielded against them, moved in for the kill. If Jesus cured this man, they had Him; for short of the bare minimum necessary to save a man's life, all medical assistance was forbidden on the Sabbath. The thoughts of the Pharisees were naked and open to the divine knowledge of Christ. With full knowledge of the consequences, the Son of Mary who had won the friendship of the strong fishermen of Galilee, now took His stand as they would have expected Him to: magnificently. He commanded the sick man to stand up where all could see him, then turning to the Pharisees, He said: "I ask you if it be lawful on the Sabbath days to do good, or to do evil; to save life, or to destroy?" (Luke 6:9). The conflict here was between a work of charity and the exaggerated observances that had been pushed to such absurdities. Jesus put the question where it belonged, on the moral level; if benefactions to a neighbor are to be forbidden, then it must be concluded that the rabbinical additions to the Law took no account of the moral law—an admission the Pharisees could not make. The moments ticked by in thick silence after the question of Jesus. As He stood there in the ominous quiet, His eyes roving over the congregation, Jesus felt the anger of a strong man and the pity of God for the hardened hearts of men. With a disregard for the Pharisees that was sharper than a blow, Jesus said to the sick man: "Stretch forth thy hand" (Mark 3:5). Instantly the divine answer to the question was given; the withered hand was restored to a healthy state.

The synagogue emptied with no further discussion. The Pharisees attempted no rebuttal to the overwhelming answer of Christ. They, too, left the synagogue but with blind fury raging in their hearts. Christ was now a hated enemy to be destroyed; and they immediately entered into consultation to effect His death. He could be denounced to the Sanhedrin in Jerusalem or to the governor of Galilee, Herod Antipas, whose permission in any case would have to be obtained. This latter court offered much quicker relief from the intolerable rebuke that Jesus was to them, so it was to the influential Jews of Herod's court that they went, driven by their murderous resentment. Herod was, indeed, quite indifferent in religious matters; but then he had neatly silenced the Baptist, perhaps he could be persuaded that the death of this other preacher of truth was to his interest. At any rate, Jesus must die.

He had ministered to men's miseries both of body and soul: cured all manner of sickness, driven out devils, forgiven sins. He had insisted on the supremacy of God over man, had come to the defense of reason in law, had made good truth's threat to unfounded claims of eminence. Through it all, divine power had been exercised in an almost reckless extravagance to confirm the truth of all that had been done and said. For this, He must die. The shock of God's presence among men does not come from His demands on them so much as His kindness to them and His mighty resistance to man's unkindness to men. It is from the love of God that men flee, for there is no answer to its uncounting generosity, but a proportionately reckless dedication that shrinks all other goods to pygmy proportions.

From this time on, the shadow of death hovered over the head of Jesus. No man believes against his will, and the enemies of Christ had no will to believe. He was a light moving through the blackness of their unbelief, but even this divine light did not dissipate the darkness. It was evident, even as early as this, that His work of saving the men of all ages would be carried on by other hands than His; for His days were numbered and His work had no limits. The welcome of men was the death of God.

✣ 7

THE CHRISTIAN CHALLENGE

IN THE quiet of an evening, Jesus left Capharnaum, walking to the nearby mountain; and there, St. Luke tells us, He passed the night in prayer. His sinless, grace-filled soul needed that converse with its Maker, as every man's soul does; at this moment, particularly, He gave us an example of a strong man advancing to crucial choices and bold truths, but not alone. When the day had dawned, He saw that His disciples had followed Him. Calling them closer, He chose twelve whom He named apostles; men chosen to be with Him and to be given the power to preach, to cast out devils, to heal the sick.

Many of them we already know. Peter, who is always named first by the Evangelists, and Andrew, his brother; James and John, the sons of Zebedee, whom He called "sons of thunder" because of temperament so violent as to be remarkable even among Galileans. These four date back to Jesus' first public appearance at the Jordan, and all four had come under the spell of the Baptist. It was on the journey back to Galilee that Philip first met Jesus, and it was he who sought out Nathanael (the Bartholomew of the apostolic lists) at his ease in Cana. Matthew was snatched from his toll booth by Christ's bald command: "follow Me." The other five enter the gospel story for the first time here in Christ's choice of them from all the men who had been following His dispersal of truth and miraculous power. There was Thomas, called the Twin, the doubting one who has such a human pull on our hearts by his stubbornness, his tardiness, and his reckless loyalty. The next named is James the son of Alphaeus; then Simon, distinguished even in that select company by his burning zeal; Judas, who is called Jude to distinguish him from the traitor, or by his surname, Thaddaeus—big-chested; all these three were cousins of Our Lord, possibly brought up in the same house with Him after the death of a parent, called anyhow, by a common Jewish usage, His brothers. Finally, and always in the last place, there is Judas Iscariot, the man from Kerioth in the south of Judaea, who was to betray Christ.

These were the new men, progenitors of a race of new men, who were to conquer the world. Their very newness, however, was still something to be accomplished; it would not be God's work alone, for it would demand from these men that they meet the challenge of that new spirit which the Son of God had come to loose upon the earth. With these chosen ones and the other disciples, Jesus came down the side of the mountain a little way to a fairly level place. Despite the early morning hour and the laborious ascent of the mountain, a very large multitude had already gathered, not merely from Galilee but from all Judaea and Jerusalem, from the sea-coast cities of Tyre and Sidon, from the Decapolis and the land beyond the Jordan. Christ was no longer merely a local celebrity, His message only a passing sensation. Here was food for the hungry, light in the darkness, and words pregnant with hope; men shirked no effort to come to Him from all corners of the land, driven by the desperation of need and enticed by the appeal of the divine.

Before this crowd, Jesus sat down; and opening His mouth He taught them. The words that came from His mouth at this moment are known to us as the Eight Beatitudes, a child's catechism lesson and a mystic's inexhaustible treasure; but at this moment, they were a description of the new men and a challenge that only the stout-hearted would attempt to meet. These were the Christian men, men of heroic quality, who would walk singing through all that life could offer in opposition, for they were the blessed ones, the happy ones; their goodness would not hang from their necks like a millstone of exaggerated piety, but would fill their hearts and overflow into the lives of all men. They would be happy men, exultantly happy, with a happiness that would reach its full bloom in eternity. The words of the Lord are short, simple, open to men of any condition who dare to face their challenge. He said:

Blessed are the the poor in spirit; for theirs is the kingdom of heaven
Blessed are the meek; for they shall possess the land.
Blessed are they that mourn; for they shall be comforted.
Blessed are they that hunger and thirst after justice; for they shall have their fill.
Blessed are the merciful; for they shall obtain mercy.
Blessed are the clean of heart; for they shall see God.
Blessed are the peacemakers; for they shall be called the children of God.

Blessed are they that suffer persecution for justice's sake; for theirs is the kingdom of heaven (Matt. 5:3–10).

A man has a strong hope of future and eternal happiness in one way because he moves with sure strides through the fine actions which win that happiness for him; in another way, because even here and now he begins to enjoy a taste of what God has stored up for him. Each of these terse sentences of the Lord states the actions by which a man merits happiness, and the share of heavenly happiness which is already his on earth and which will be perfected in heaven. The poverty mentioned here has nothing to do with lack or abundance of riches, but with a heart courageous enough to refuse to be enslaved. Meekness is no relative of weakness, but the quality of a man who holds the strongest of the passions under a firm rein. The mourning are not those engulfed in self-pity, but the wise ones who weep for the abuse they and others have made of the gifts and the creatures of God. Those famished for justice are not the champions of their own rights, but men aflame with concern for others. The merciful are not the sentimental who offer the doubtful comfort of their slobbering, but men rich enough in goodness and generous enough to fill up the emptiness of another's misery from their own God-given abundance. The clean of heart are not the prudes, but the men whose minds live on the clean air of truth and whose affections, consequently, are strangers to the enemies of innocence. The peacemakers are not reformers sharply observant of the sins of others, but men who are masters of themselves, men whose perfectly ordered lives flood their own souls with peace in such abundance that it overflows into the lives of those about them. The martyrs, victims of persecution, are the men who, having first things so firmly first in their own lives, are not to be cajoled or threatened into surrendering the least of those priceless first things. Christ's description of the activity of these new and happy men, in other words, is by no means an absurdly idyllic picture of pious weaklings snivelling their way through the world of stronger men; rather, He asks of men more than the strongest heart can find in itself to give. Christ was not a revolutionary, full of false promises of immediate and tangible rewards of loot, asking of men only that they throw over all laws and strike down their fellows. His demands fell on the individual, His prescription called for a man's violence to be directed against the disorders in the kingdom of his own soul; His rewards were things to be had, not by snatching them from the hands of others, but by cultivating them within a man's own soul.

The men of Our Lord's age, as of our own and, indeed, of every age, fixed their hearts on happiness and dedicated all their waking hours to an indefatigable pursuit of it. In His time, as in ours, men exhausted the possibilities in their choice of a life that promised happiness: some sought it in a voluptuous life, some in a life of whirling activity, still others in a quiet life of contemplation. The first holds out a completely false promise, is an insult to reason itself, and is bitterly degrading to a man. It is rather an impediment to happiness than a bestowal of it. The happy man, then, proceeds to remove this impediment: a man poor in spirit goes beyond moderate use of riches and honors to a complete freedom from their enticement; he achieves tranquillity in the face of the violence of his passions of attack and defense, and so is meek; in place of pleasure's invitation to abuse of the good things God has made, he is ready, if necessary, to forswear these pleasures altogether. The active life, rightly lived, is a disposition to happiness, for it consists precisely in filling the lives of our neighbors with what is their due and what is our gift. The happy man who dares to follow Christ does more than surrender to another what is his due, he is on fire in this regard, as eager as a hungry man for food or a thirsty man for water. He goes beyond the demands of liberality in his gifts, beyond the spontaneous generosity that cares so thoughtfully for those who are friends, relatives, parts of himself by some link or another; for him, no greater incentive to generosity is necessary than the needs of another, any other, for he is the merciful man whose reward shall be mercy. The contemplative life, which is the life of heaven, begins on this earth when a man begins to touch on his own perfection with a consequent cleanness of mind and of heart, when his relations with his neighbors are a constant echo of the peace flooding his own heart, when, in comparison with the divine invitations, all other values are easily, even joyfully, surrendered that this one might be saved.

The patient wisdom of Christ recognized the validity of the desires of men, even of the most mistaken of men. The light of that wisdom, turned on the kinds of life that men embraced, picked out the good in each and held it before the eyes of these new, happy men as an immediate reward. The voluptuous man makes his mistake in seeking the satisfaction of his desires outside of God; the happy man, on the same search, but in God, finds all that the mistaken man so desires and so completely misses. Those who fix on honors and riches as their goal are really seeking a kind of excellence and abundance; both of these are had in the kingdom of

God promised to the poor in spirit and beginning on this earth. Fierce men, through their quarrels and wars, seek security through the destruction of their enemies; this security is promised to the meek in their quiet, undisturbed possession both of the human goods in life and the eternal goods in heaven. The voluptuaries who plunge into the pleasures of the flesh and the softly enervating embrace of the world are really frightened and lonely men seeking consolation for the difficulties and labors of human living; this is the consolation promised to those brave enough to admit mistakes and regret them. Men cheat themselves of the happiness that should properly be theirs from the active life's concern for neighbor when, through an exaggerated caution lest they themselves be empty-handed, they violate all justice in seizing the goods of others. To the happy men of Christ, strangers to such caution, it is promised that they shall indeed not be empty-handed but shall have their fill. If loss of this active life's happiness is from defect of mercy, it is from fear of touching even the ragged garment of another man's misery, as though misery were a kind of contagion they dared not risk. Against this, the Lord promises the merciful, not indeed that they shall avoid all misery, but that they in their turn will find the mercy that fills the gnawing emptiness of misery. The happiness of the contemplative needs no reform or changing, nothing more indeed than the full bloom to this life's present bud: so the clean of heart, seeing better for that very cleanness, are to receive the full vision of God which is eternal life; the peacemakers, so clearly the images of the God of unity and peace, are rightly called the sons of God made in His image.

The rewards promised by the Lord in the Beatitudes are not mutually exclusive prizes, not disparate goods of which this or that man may get one or another. They are a cumulative blessedness that ascends to a crescendo of heavenly harmony within the soul of a man. It is much more to possess the land of the kingdom of heaven than merely to have it, for we have many things which we do not firmly and peacefully possess. It is still a greater thing to be consoled in that kingdom than to have and possess it, for we possess many things in sorrow. Again, it is more to have one's fill than simply to be comforted, for fullness implies abundance of comfort. Mercy surpasses satiety for through mercy a man receives more than he merited, indeed more than he could have thought to desire. It is yet a higher bliss to see God, and at the top of the scale to hold the high place of the sons of God.

In giving His picture of the new men, the demands made on their virtue and the rewards piling up beyond the dreams of men, Christ had been speaking as from a professor's chair, content to let the incisive wisdom of His words stand by itself. Now, in a confidential tone and speaking in the second person directly to the disciples, He gives them words of strength and consolation; they will need it, for it is precisely such men, a living rebuke to the waywardness of the worldly, who will most surely suffer persecution precisely because they deserve it the least. "Blessed are ye when they shall revile you, and persecute you, and speak all that is evil against you, untruly, for My sake. Be glad and rejoice, for your reward is very great in heaven. For so they persecuted the prophets that were before you" (Matt. 5:11–12). They are to rejoice, not in spite of the persecutions but because of them, for to men suffering in His name persecution becomes a kind of accolade; a recognition by the world of the sterling and complete opposition of the new spirit of Christ to that of the world.

So it had happened to the prophets; so it would be to these new leaders of a New Law. With this prophetic tribute to the great eminence of the twelve He had just chosen, Christ launched into the discourse that has come down to us as the Sermon on the Mount. The Beatitudes, breathing the challenging spirit that was to renovate the world, served as an admirable introduction to the contrast He was now about to make between the Old and the New Law. "Do not think that I am come to destroy the Law, or the prophets. I am not come to destroy but to fulfill. For amen I say unto you, till heaven and earth pass, one jot, or one tittle shall not pass of the law, till all be fulfilled. . . . For I tell you, that unless your justice abound more than that of the scribes and Pharisees, you shall not enter into the kingdom of heaven" (Matt.5:17–18, 20). He put the high demands of the New Law positively in His insistence that His disciples "become perfect as your heavenly Father is perfect," a thing impossible until the fulfillment of the Old Law.

It was, of course, the moral precepts of the ancient law that were the subject of fulfillment by Our Lord; the ceremonial precepts, centering in the temple sacrifices, were in fact superseded by the new sacrifice of the divine Victim, and the judicial precepts gave way to those of the New Law whose formulation was left by Christ to apostolic leaders carrying on His work through the ages. His concern here was the moral law which directs and perfects the soul of a man; that law was to be fulfilled in the only way in which truth can be fulfilled: by clearer statement, deeper penetration, and increasingly fruitful effects. Since the goal of the moral law, the perfection of man, is necessarily unchangeable, not one jot or tittle of the essential precepts of that law could be changed. But the seed of love of God and neighbor, sown in the Old Law, was, in the New, to be brought to full maturity and fill the world with its perfume.

Before the eyes of the men gathered on the mountain about the seated Christ in the clear freshness of a summer morning, an upset world righted itself as the words poured from His lips. The world, both physical and social, which had dwarfed men into insignificance by its massiveness, shrunk to the size of a tool in a man's hand before the grandeur of the image of God; nor was this a dreamer's program for the destruction of the wickedness of the world or the world of wickedness, but a divine realist's demand that men live in a world in conflict, themselves holding an invulnerable mastery of their own souls. Men enmeshed in a web of precepts of an external religion that dictated every step, every lift of their hand, every detail of their living with all the sanctions of religious authority, suddenly found themselves free to love God and neighbor, to live both humanly and divinely. Now their every step, every lift of their hand, every breath of their days, every detail of their living, would be God's, not by the dictation of precept, but by the dedication of love. The Old Law contained only the seed rich in promise, the New Law contained and demanded the full fruit. The Old Law had been rendered impossible by the artificial complexities woven into it by men; the New Law, divinely difficult by its very grandeur, is as simple as the act by which a man throws his heart away.

It was easy for these men, the very simplest of them,

to follow the conclusions drawn by Christ from the fundamental principle of the New Law. Emphasis on externals might be satisfied to forbid murder, but love in a man's heart would be intolerant even of anger. Prohibition of adultery would satisfy concern for the externals, but reverence for the imaged dignity and beauty of a loved God cannot be patient of the least thought of impurity. It is not enough for one in love with God to refrain from perjury's abuse of the loved one's name, such a man must treat the divine name with uncommon care, using it sparingly in confirmation of his own words. An eye for an eye is adequate measure where only justice is in question; where love enters in, there is happiness enough in a man's heart to minister to the misery of another's sin by the balm of forgiveness.

Indeed, as far as external actions were concerned, the precepts of Christ throughout all of His public teaching were very few. It could hardly have been otherwise. The core of the New Law is the grace of God, by which men come alive to God, manifested in faith working through love. Men acquire this life-giving grace through the Son of God made man. That grace was given in Galilee by a few simple words: "Be of good heart, son, thy sins are forgiven thee." In the years when Christ walked no more among men, it came from Him through the instruments He left for that purpose, the sacraments. There was, then, no need for external precepts beyond those inducing to grace, the sacraments, and those relating to acts produced from the instinct of grace or levelled in its protection. In actual fact we find no other exterior works commanded beyond the sacraments and the moral precepts which of themselves pertain to the essence of virtue. Beyond that, the heart of man is invited to works as high and hard as the heights of God; but invited, not driven.

In the simple words that flowed from His mouth as He sat and taught them on the mountain, Christ gave these eager men the whole information on Christian life, the whole program for the perfect ordering of the interior actions of men; and thereby showed men for all time the place of the world beneath a man and the sovereign invulnerability of man's own kingdom. The first step in that perfect ordering which initiates happiness on earth and guarantees it in heaven has to do with a man himself. He has things to do irrespective of the world or his fellows: he has good to get done, evil to be avoided, not only in the externals visible to men, but in the interior regions that are known only to God and himself. He has, in other words, to follow the directions of the moral precepts, indeed to protect those precepts in himself by avoiding even the occasions of their violations. In the good he does, his aim is not to lay up treasure either in the minds or the marts of men; he is not seeking human glory, but the glory of God and his own eternal happiness. If all this is true within himself, then by easy consequence, his relations with his neighbor will be as they should: he will not judge his neighbor temerariously, unjustly, presumptuously; on the other hand, neither will he be so naively careless as to commit sacred things to an unworthy neighbor, casting pearls before swine. It will not be enough for a man merely to hear this new word, to confess his faith in it, nor work miracles in His name; he must do the things that love of God and neighbor demand of his heart. The task is not one that a man approaches, swaggeringly confident of his own strength. Only a fool would expect to succeed without a constant divine aid; surely a wise man would be instant in his prayer for that assistance, cautious in his protection of this love from seducers, humbly loyal in his adherence to the commandments that show him the way, careful in his realization of the narrowness of the path and the door that opens on happiness.

The Pharisees had made much of almsgiving, of prayer, and of fasting; these things were, indeed, their badge of honor publicly worn in open search for the approval and appreciation of men. Many a man listening there to Christ on the mountain could well have had his fill of such dividend-paying piety, and be revolted by the works themselves because of the men and the manner of their doing them. As divine wisdom revealed their true beauty, these works took a new hold on the hearts of men. Fasting is as wide as all the things a man does by way of curbing his selfishness, almsgiving is a generosity as all-embracing as the things a man does for love of his neighbor, and prayer is a word that covers all that a man does in worship of God. Obviously, none of these are done to puff a man up, none of them are held out as bait to a flatterer, none of them look to the applause of men; but all of them spring from and look to the God in whose name a man finds strength to get them done. So understood, it is these three that lead a man to his happiness and turn him away from the misery awaiting him who puts his happiness in carnal pleasure, riches, and honors.

The audience of Christ, too, harbored the eternal hunger for happiness that drives men through each day, and no doubt many of them had been the victims of the false promises which were all that the world of their time had to offer. Even with the divine prescription for happiness in their hands, they would still have to live in the world of temporalities and use the greater part of each day laboring for those very things which a man must have, yet which he embraces to his own destruction. About these things a man must think, he must be provident, he must plan and labor. No one would know that better than the son of the carpenter of Nazareth; and none would know better how to deal with those pressing needs than the Son of God, who was born of Mary. There is a ring of complete authenticity in the thoughtfulness that moved Christ, here in the midst of the beauty of divine truths, to stoop to the common needs of men; from His human experience, the love of His heart, and the wisdom of His divinity, He warned men away from the anxieties that could bring disaster. Granted the need of temporal things, no man should make them his goal, dedicate his life to them, or serve his God because of them; laying up treasure to the point where he has no time to live. Whatever the pressure of those needs, no man is justified in despair of obtaining them; for surely our heavenly Father knows we have need of them, and He is truly a Father watching over His children. No matter how high we ride on the flood of prosperity, let no man suppose he is self-sufficient; against the temptation to pride, let him try to add one cubit to his stature. The evil of any day is sufficient for a man's concern; the future is God's and only the man who scorns God has reason to fear it.

As the lesson ended, Jesus returned with His disciples to Capharnaum. The men who had listened to Him went down the mountain with their minds reeling from the impact of divine wisdom given in words so clear and so divinely simple. Even human prudence would declare that it was a fitting time for following up that kindly blow in confirmation and still further illumination of the feeble minds of men. Men's weakness makes them quick and easy admirers of power, and there is little by way of refutation to offer a naked show of the power of God; so, with divine wisdom, there was little delay between the return to Capharnaum and the manifestation of divine power through miracles.

Our Lord was approached in Capharnaum by friendly envoys of a Roman centurion, a pagan. His upright life, generous heart, and searching mind were attested by his kindness to the subject Jews, his respect for their religion, and his deep concern for the welfare of one of his servants who lay in great pain, seriously ill. He had heard of the wonders worked by Jesus, had pondered the reports that came to him of the teaching of this man who had awakened all of Galilee. At his request, some of the upright men of the town approached Jesus with the request that He come and heal the servant of so worthy a man. Immediately agreeing, Jesus set off for the centurion's house. Meanwhile, the Roman officer had had time to think: if the ordinary Jew could not enter his house without incurring ritual impurity, what of this man whose sanctity was a byword in the countryside; indeed, perhaps this was not merely a man, who exercised such sovereignty over the physical universe. In hurried humility, he sent some of his friends just in time to catch Jesus not far from the house; they carried a message of faith, reverence, humility so precious that it has ever since been repeated every time the Lord enters the house of a man's soul in Holy Communion. "Lord, trouble not thyself; for I am not worthy that thou shouldest enter under my roof. For which cause neither did I think myself worthy to come to thee; but say the word, and my servant shall be healed. For I also am a man subject to authority, having under me soldiers: and I say to one, Go, and he goeth; and to another, Come, and he cometh; and to my servant, Do this, and he doth it" (Luke 7:6–8). It was a faith worthy of the admiration and praise given it by Christ; the servant was healed at this moment, and the wonder that had struck the men of Capharnaum in Christ's first appearance in their synagogue was underlined and made explicit: He spoke with authority, divine authority, an authority easily recognized even by a pagan.

We next find Jesus at the gate of the little town of Naim, southwest of Nazareth, about seven or eight hours walk from Capharnaum, and nearly opposite Mt. Thabor. He had been on the road with His disciples, and a very great crowd followed Him. As they approached the gate, a mourning procession came out on its way to the burial of the only son of a widow of that little town. No word was said, no favor asked. Jesus went directly to the bereft mother, "moved with mercy towards her," to say the words we say so helplessly in empty attempts at comfort: "Don't cry." "And He came near and touched the bier. And they that carried it stood still. And He said: Young man, I say to thee, arise. And he that was dead, sat up, and began to speak. And He gave him to his mother" (Luke 7:14–15). Fear fell on the whole great crowd, and they glorified God, recognizing that a great prophet had risen up among them, and God had visited His people. The word spread like wildfire, following on the centurion's recognition of the authority of Christ; it went the length and breadth of the country and men wondered to each other, as the centurion had to himself, whether this man could be merely a man.

The disciples of John the Baptist had kept him informed of the teaching and miracles of Jesus. Though the precursor still languished in his mountain prison east of the Dead Sea, a long way from Galilee, he soon heard of this call of the dead to life which was such a sensation throughout the land. His response was quite different from that of the crowd who had witnessed the miracle; they were being slowly awakened, whereas John had been taught of God and had recognized the Son of Mary as Him Who was to come, at His first appearance by the Jordan. John had no doubts; but his imprisonment had taken nothing from his strong soul and fiery temperament. He was impatient at the pace of Christ, eager for the striking appearance of the judge who would give justice and mete out punishment. He waited for the thundering condemnations of the Messias to shake the land out of its lethargy; yet he heard reports only of patiently gradual teaching, of a flood of kindly use of divine power, of divine authority exercised not against men but for them.

With the familiarity that is deep affection's right, he sent two of his disciples with the cryptic message that would make his impatience plain to the Lord: "Art Thou He that art to come; or look we for another?" (Luke 7:19). In the very hour in which the messengers came to Him, the Lord "cured many of their diseases, and hurts, and evil spirits; and to many that were blind He gave sight." The answer given for John to his disciples was more than a reference to the miracles happening under their eyes; they were words that John himself could not misunderstand, for they were almost a paraphrase of Isaias' description of the day of the Messias: "Go and relate to John what you have heard and seen: the blind see, the lame walk, the lepers are made clean, the deaf hear, the dead rise again, to the poor the gospel is preached." This last phrase, too, Christ had applied to Himself in the first reading of the

Scriptures in the synagogue of His own Nazareth. The assurance Jesus sent to John was that the reign of the Messias had indeed begun; but the working out of that kingdom must be left to the Lord to do in His own divinely gentle way, a way that would not overwhelm men, not terrorize them, but win their hearts.

When the messengers had gone their way with the response, Jesus turned to the crowd to speak plainly the praises of John: a prophet, and more than a prophet, the very precursor of the Messias foretold by the prophets, the last of the great figures of the Old Testament. His mission fused into that of Jesus, for the Old and the New Testaments are not opposed, but a divine unity; yet it is the Old which is subordinate, and John, as a part of that Old dispensation, is historically subordinate to the least in the new kingdom. The common people and the publicans, who now were welcoming Christ, heard John and embraced his baptism; but the Pharisees and the scribes despised the counsel of God and rejected John's baptism as they were rejecting his Master's teaching. "And the Lord said: Whereunto then shall I liken the men of this generation? And to what are they like? They are like to children sitting in the market place, and speaking one to another saying: We have piped to you and you have not danced: we have mourned, and you have not wept. For John the Baptist came neither eating bread nor drinking wine; and you say: He hath a devil. The Son of man is come eating and drinking; and you say: Behold a man that is a glutton and a drinker of wine, a friend of publicans and sinners. And wisdom is justified by all her children" (Luke 7:31–35). Both dispensations were rejected by the men who would not hear the man who said: "Behold the Lamb of God" and would not follow the Chosen One so clearly pointed out by the precursor.

In these incidents, the person of the Messias begins to emerge as quietly yet as clearly as a mountain peak when the morning sun unwraps the veiling of mist that hid it. The pagan centurion had seen the sovereign sway of Jesus and was humbled before it; the whole country was startled at the gentleness and power that gave the widow back her son; John's messengers brought back the precursor's ringing words to the minds of men, and the Lord's answer called the prophets to witness the divine reality of His mission. An incident now occurred that was the occasion for Our Lord Himself to declare the wonders of His person gently but clearly.

Simon, a Pharisee of Galilee yet with some kindly feeling towards Jesus, invited Him to dinner. The invitation was well meant, but, with the prejudices of his class, Simon could not shake off all restraint; he was courteous but cool, correct in his attention to his guest but no more than just correct. As they reclined at table in the manner of the time, on low couches laid out from the table, a woman stepped out from the crowd of onlookers and, approaching the couch of Jesus, knelt by His feet. The other guests and the onlookers could see the alabaster vase of perfumed oil, and could guess her intention, as she knelt by His feet, of anointing His feet with the precious oil. Only God could know the desperate courage in the heart of the woman and the enveloping shame as she exposed herself to the scorn of all, for everyone knew her as a public sinner. As she knelt stooping over the Lord's feet, the courage that had steeled her against the scorn of men broke. The tears poured from her eyes over the feet of Christ; shamed, confused, a little panicked at the breakdown of her graceful gesture, she hastily loosened her hair and wiped at the tears though they flowed faster than she could wipe them away. Finally, she let her heart take over; bending down, she kissed His feet, and poured the precious oil on them.

Simon, watching his guest, had seen no slightest sign of shock, revulsion, or even of disapproval on the face of Jesus; surely, he thought, if this man were a prophet, he would know what kind of a woman it was who touched him. Jesus knew more than that; He knew what went on in the mind and heart of Simon. After the little parable that brought from Simon the considered judgment that the debtor who was forgiven most loved his benefactor most, the Lord in His turn poured precious ointment on the heart of all the sinners of all the ages. "Turning to the woman, He said unto Simon: Dost thou see this woman? I entered into thy house, thou gavest me no water for my feet; but she with tears hath washed my feet, and with her hairs hath wiped them. Thou gavest me no kiss; but she, since she came in, hath not ceased to kiss my feet. My head with oil thou didst not anoint; but she with ointment hath anointed my feet. Wherefore I say to thee: Many sins are forgiven her, because she hath loved much. But to whom less is forgiven, he loveth less. And He said to her: Thy sins are forgiven thee. And they that sat at meat with Him began to say within themselves: Who is this that forgiveth sins also? And He said to the woman: Thy faith hath made thee safe, go in peace" (Luke 7:44–50). There is almost a brusqueness in the total disregard of Christ for the unspoken protests of His dinner companions, a definite tenderness in His further gifts to the woman: not only are her sins forgiven her, she is safe, she has peace.

The interior mutterings at this man forgiving sin had their justification; if this were mere man, His pretensions were blasphemous. But here in this very scene, He made it clear that He was indeed much more than man. It has always been known that perfect love wins forgiveness of sins, that an act of perfect contrition is really no more than an act of love salted by tears of regret; but the love must be love of God, not love of man. Man is saved by faith, but by faith in God's word, not faith in any man. This woman, soiled by shame, and without attempting excuse for her past, came to Jesus: it was Christ she loved, Christ in Whom she had faith, it was to Christ that she looked for the cleansing of her soul and the peace of God in her heart. If that love could forgive sin, then clearly it was God she was loving in loving the Son of Mary. She had come to the only One with a welcome for a sinner; to the One in whom every sinner would always find a home, safe, peaceful, sinless.

✣ 8

THE LITTLE ONES

THE divine concern for the least of men, for the obscure, the forgotten, the despised, becomes the dominant note of the days that immediately follow the scene in the house of Simon. It almost seems as if these days were a continued, vivid, living response to the Baptist's fiery expectations of crashing judgments and quick, decisive victory by almighty power. By contrast, a thread of tenderness runs through these days, thoughtful of men's weakness, patient of their slowness, forgiving of their sins, alert to the value of the most neglected; yet with no trace of weakness or flabby compromise. He was come, not to judge but to save; and to save not only Israel, but all the world of men.

The tiny villages and obscure localities were reached by the preaching journeys, now become more and more systematic. The seed of organization began to sprout in the Lord's own little band which took on steadily a more permanent form. St. Luke's words allow us to look into the womb of that present to see the embryo of the Church in the process of being born. "He travelled through the cities and towns, preaching and evangelizing the kingdom of God; and the twelve with Him: and certain women who had been healed of evil spirits and infirmities; Mary, who is called Magdalen, out of whom seven devils were gone forth, and Joanna, the wife of Chusa, Herod's steward, and Susanna, and many others who ministered unto Him of their substance" (Luke 8:1–3). Here we see the Master and Lord; the specially chosen ones who are to share and carry on His work with His authority; and the ministration indispensable for labors so constant as to preclude a man supporting himself by his own hands. These women were grateful to Christ: grateful for His merciful gifts of health, of release from the slavery of the devil, of forgiveness of sin; or simply grateful for His goodness. It is the way of God to be patient of gratitude's longing to utter itself in action. Here we see Christ taking on the humbler and harder role of recipient of the gifts of men, even putting Himself and His apostles at the mercy of the ministration of these women for the very essentials of food and clothing.

Some of these women would have means; but not all, for they did much more than offer gifts of money. It was their delight to set the Lord and His apostles free to do the impossibly divine things that had been done for them and must be done for others. Mary Magdalen, found so early in this company, plainly had reasons for enduring gratitude to the Lord. The phrase of the Evangelist that seven devils had been cast out of her indicates not merely release from diabolic possession, but from a relapsed state of possession, from a state into which Magdalen had fallen again after having once been freed; a condition that might well argue, too, to serious moral lapses, though not necessarily so. At any rate, she has won the heart of all Christendom by the burning love and utter loyalty she gave to Him Who had snatched her from the devil. Sanctity and its reward of heaven, love and loyalty, a gratitude that never tires of saying thanks, are all in Magdalen's story, a story that has ever since been an inspiration, a tower of strength, and a personally cherished tale of exquisite beauty for every Christian. Scholars do not agree on the identification of Mary Magdalen with the sinful woman of Simon's feast and with Mary of Bethany, the sister of Martha. Some have held that all three were really one and the same person, though the gospel story describes Magdalen as a woman of the north, Mary the sister of Martha as a woman of the south; still the opinion does not lack probability and has had a hearty welcome through the ages. On the other hand, it could well be that these were three distinct women, each with her own heart-filling reasons for gratitude, love, and loyalty to Christ. Of the three, Mary Magdalen and the sinful woman of Simon's feast seem much more nearly of the same recklessly generous temperament; if there is to be identity traced between these women, surely it is Magdalen and the repentant sinner who are one and the same. It was such a woman who was most likely to minister to her divine benefactor through all the days of His preaching and teaching, to follow Him to Calvary, stay to the end in the midst of the hostile mob on Calvary, even to carry her ministry beyond His death to His tomb.

Not that these women were all with the apostolic band all the time; arrangements would be made between them to assure the constant womanly service that was so necessary to the untrammeled work of preaching and teaching. Nor, in fact, was this apostolic group on the road every day and all day. Capharnaum was the center from which they made their sorties and to which they returned. It was such a return to the city that St.

Mark signals (3:20, 31–35) when he tells of the affectionate concern of the family or clan of Jesus. Such a crowd had gathered in and about the house in which they were that they had not so much as time to eat; not an unusual thing in view of the pressure of their days. In fact, it happened so often that the rumor of it filtered back to Nazareth and to the scattered members of the family; to the facts were added wild rumors of physical and mental breakdown which roused the concern of these who were so close to Him by blood. In the East then, as now, it was the family, rather than the town or the city, to which a man belonged, which took responsibility for his errors, credit for his accomplishments, and anxious concern for his welfare. Driven by these rumors, the responsible members of the clan gathered and went to Capharnaum, Mary of course among them; not because she would have any uneasiness on her own part, but because her presence would be demanded on such a mission, and, too, because her heart would need no urging to seize upon a chance to go to her Son.

"And His mother and His brethren came; and standing without, sent unto Him, calling Him. And the multitude sat about Him; and they said to Him: Behold thy mother and thy brethren without seek for Thee." The answer of Christ held nothing of displeasure, no hint of reproach for this affectionate family concern; rather in full appreciation of this family love, Christ invited all men to share an even deeper, more intimate, more steadfastly loyal family bond. "And answering them, He said: Who is my mother and my brethren? And looking round about on them who sat about Him, He saith: Behold my mother and my brethren. For whosoever shall do the will of God, he is my brother, and my sister, and my mother."

"The same day Jesus going out of the house, sat by the sea side" (Matt. 13:1). ". . . and a great multitude was gathered together unto Him, so that He went up into a ship, and sat in the sea; and all the multitude was upon the land by the sea side. And He taught them many things in parables" (Mark 4:1–2). St. Matthew here records eight of these parables couched in words of such simple beauty and dignity as to make it difficult to tear our eyes away from them; yet we miss the greater beauty, and the strong tenderness that brought forth the beauty, if we do not see the circumstances that framed these masterpieces. The Sermon on the Mount was sharply clear, forcing the mind to decisive acceptance or rejection; the parables, on the contrary, have their full beauty veiled, their meaning is to be ferreted out by the mind, caught up by the clues given, the familiarity of the material, and the implicit promises of treasures hidden in the figurative speech. The obscurity was deliberate; but it was by no means a petty mind's instrument of niggardliness or the tantalizing patronage of a proudly superior mind. The very obscurity was a statement, in fact, of the patient concern of Christ for the least of men, an example of the most difficult of all the varieties of patience, that intellectual patience which slows the steps of wisdom's words to the pace of a stumbling mind. The Sermon on the Mount developed the theme that had been familiar to men through all the rabbinical teaching: that righteousness is demanded of man for his salvation, that God is first in mind and heart, that love goes out beyond the furthest reaches of justice. Men would have no difficulty receiving such teaching however great their reluctance in living it. The doctrine of the parables had no such easy sailing; before it could receive a welcome from these men, an old, deeply cherished, fiercely held illusion had to be cleared from the mind of men. The parables spoke of the kingdom of heaven, the redemption by the Messias which had been the hope of Israel for so many centuries. These men, and their masters, saw it as a lightning stroke, confounding their enemies in a moment while they were lifted to triumphant heights of glory without delay, without effort, in a moment's application of almighty power. Gently, patiently, delicately, the Lord set about removing this cancer of false hope from the minds and hearts of His listeners.

Direct argument could not cut through the stubbornness of these minds. Christ's method was the method of the parables. Each one holds out promise of hidden riches to the searching mind; with a subtlety that is yet utterly simple, each mind is drawn into taking its own steps away from error and towards the truth by pondering the familiar things now packed with meaning. No one could live in Galilee of that time and be unfamiliar with such things of the farm as the sower and the fate of his hand-scattered seed, the slow but inexorable ripening of the grain, the threat to the wheat from the cockle. Every pilgrim, in a land where everyone was a pilgrim at least once in the year, would have seen both the tiny mustard seed and its prodigious product; every housewife would know the power of leaven. In Palestine, even in recent years and certainly in the time of Christ, the one hope of safety for valuables in troubled times was a secret burial of them; treasure might well be found in any field, and many of the listeners of Christ would have taken that means to safeguard their possessions. These men, sitting by the sea shore listening to Christ's voice coming across the water from the little boat, would know well about the pearls merchants were so eager to buy, and the nets dragged in from shallow water with their miscellaneous catch.

These were the familiar, homely things into which Our Lord wrapped the truth of the kingdom of heaven. It was not to come to men without effort on their part; the seed could fall on barren ground, could be snatched from minds and hearts, choked by cares and enticements. The interior dispositions of men were as crucial as is the soil to the sown seed. The kingdom would not come in an instant, and no amount of patriotic hoping would hurry it any more than a farmer's impatience hurries the harvest; rather it comes in God's good time and, in a sense, inch by inch, much as the grain creeps to maturity through the seasons. It would not be an instantaneous crushing of enemies and glorification of Israel; time and patience were of its essence, the good would continue mixed with the evil as the cockle with the wheat. Time and patience; but the thing was sure, inexorably sure; as at the harvest, so at the judgment of men there would be separation of the cockle to destruction, of the wheat to security. The kingdom of heaven would not appear before the eyes of men with a crash of thunder and a blaze of lightning, there would be no trumpets blown, no triumphant chariots running ahead with the news of victory. It would begin, in itself and in each man's heart, humbly, almost insignificantly, as small as the mustard seed; but with the same almost incredible magnitude in its ultimate fullness. It is a touch of yeast leavening the whole mass of a man's life, of a man's world.

Dreams of a rush of victory, of quick and easy reward, of a glory coming upon men like a tidal wave, must give way to the facts of the kingdom of heaven: facts of patience, of slow-moving time, of untiring effort, of humble beginnings and serene hope of things beyond the dreams of men. But it is worth all that a man can give for its gain; if the finder of treasure will hurry out to buy up the field, the merchant rush to buy the pearl of great price, both selling all to achieve these precious things, how much more does the kingdom of God demand of men and promise to them? But there must be patience. It is not to come at the end of the world. Rather, it is already started; and there is reason to wonder, not that it is not already perfect, but that God gave such gifts to men. There will be a time for final reckoning; the men of the world will be seined from the universe as fishes from the sea, and then it will be time to separate the good from the bad, to come at last upon the full perfection of the kingdom and the joy of its eternal possession.

All these things the Lord gave to the crowds in the obscurity of parables. In no other way could they have been made to take these truths, and in this way each one could take as much as he would in his pondering penetration of the truth. With the apostles, it was a different matter. To them it was given to know, not only the general truths, but also the mysteries of the kingdom of heaven. Theirs was a great privilege. "Blessed are your eyes, because they see, and your ears, because they hear. For amen I say to you, many prophets and just men have desired to see the things that you see, and have not seen them, to hear the things that you hear and have not heard them" (Matt. 13:16–17). In private, the Lord explained in detail the parables of the sower and of the cockle. But this was not merely for the disciples alone; they were apostles, men dedicated to teaching as the Master had taught, to bringing the kingdom of heaven into the hearts of men, and the souls of men into the kingdom of God. If their privileges were great, no less were their responsibilities. "And He said to them: Doth a candle come in to be put under a bushel, or under a bed, and not to be set on a candlestick? For there is nothing hid which shall not be made manifest: neither was it made secret, but that it may come abroad. . . . Take heed what you hear. In what measure you shall mete, it shall be measured to you again, and more shall be given to you" (Mark 4:21–22, 24). "Have ye understood all these things? They say to Him: Yes. He said unto them: Therefore every scribe instructed in the kingdom of heaven is like to a man that is a householder who bringeth forth out of his treasure new things and old" (Matt. 13:51–52).

When the last parable had been spoken on that day of special tenderness, Jesus took the disciples by surprise. "And He saith to them that day, when evening was come: Let us pass over to the other side. And sending away the multitude, they take Him even as He was in the ship" (Mark 4:35–36). Hitherto, the preaching and miracles had taken place in Galilee; now, on a moment's notice, the disciples were told to make for the pagan land across the Lake of Tiberias. Their obedience was so instant that they took Jesus, just as He was, with no provision against the chill of the night or the cutting wind of a storm from the north. As they launched out into the deep, Jesus, who was a carpenter, not a sailor, curled up on a cushion in the stern of the boat and promptly fell asleep. As every teacher or preacher knows, He had well earned that sleep, for to bring wisdom to men their masters must give something of themselves as well as all of the truth. Jesus was tired and His sleep so profound that even the tossing boat and hurtling waves did not disturb Him. In ordinary circumstances, the crossing of the lake would have been no great matter to these men of the sea who were handling the boat; but a north wind funneled through the narrow gap at the head of the lake whipped its shallow waters into a frenzy threatening enough to terrify men who knew every whim and caprice of the sea. The waves broke over the ship; it was taking water badly; this was a crisis that called for more than seamanship. The disciples did what every seasoned sailor does in just such circumstances; they appealed not to other sailors but to the Master of the sea. "And they came and awaked Him, saying: Master, we perish" (Luke 8:24). "And rising up, He rebuked the wind, and said to the sea: Peace, be still. And the wind ceased: and there was made a great calm. And He said to them: Why are you fearful? Have you not faith yet?" (Mark 4:39–40). They had had faith, surely; their appeal had not been to His knowledge of the sea but to His mastery of it. But not faith enough to keep fear at bay by the knowledge of His presence. Now they had a better reason for a healthier fear, the fear of men in the presence of Almighty God. "And they feared exceedingly: and they said one to another: Who is this (thinkest thou) that both wind and sea obey Him?" (Mark 4:40). He did indeed speak as one having authority, authority enough to put peace in the sea and reverent terror in the hearts of men.

Normally, the crossing of the lake would take about two hours. The storm would certainly cause some delay; but the party had set out in the evening and did not land on the opposite shore until full daylight. The men in these ships were, after all, fishermen, and night was the time for fishing on a lake where a broiling sun ruled the day. Undoubtedly they had intended to spend most of the night at their trade when they had set sail so early in the evening. When they landed in the country of the Gerasens—really in the neighborhood of the town of Koursi—there was no difficulty about a beach to land on; indeed, the place is still frequented by fishermen. There is a fair beach running up to the rocky heights that dominate the not far distant town, and the rocks are honeycombed with small caves which might well be used for tombs or for dwelling places for the destitute. One of these caves had been seized upon as a refuge for one who had become a terror to his fellowmen and an agony to himself. Possessed by the devil, he wandered these desolate stretches naked, bruising and cutting his body, defeating with a superhuman strength all attempts to bind him; fierce, despoiled of everything, even to the use of his mind and control of his actions, he seemed hardly more than a dangerous brute living in savage unrest. It was this creature who rushed at Jesus in brutal ferocity as He stepped from the boat.

For those who do not believe in demons, the story of this encounter has little meaning; but that will be the fate of any set of facts at the hands of those who do not read the meaning of the facts but rather write the meaning of their errors into the facts. To dismiss the established historicity of the gospel story by a wave of the hand, and in the same gesture annihilate the current evidence of malignant activity beyond human powers in the world of men, gives much the same petty illusion of power as that achieved by the man who blots out the sun by covering his eyes. Some of these disbelievers are even stupid enough to deny the existence of God, finding the mystery of His infinite nature too much for them while they swallow with relish the contradiction of a world giving birth to itself. The devil himself makes no such mistakes. The possessed man's mad rush stopped short, his fierce cries were silenced as he came to Jesus and threw himself at the feet of the Lord. "And crying with a loud voice, he said: What have I to do with thee, Jesus the Son of the most high God? I adjure thee by God that thou torment me not. For He said unto him: Go out of the man, thou unclean spirit" (Mark 5:7–8).

The divine wisdom of Christ had known at once that this man's condition was not madness but diabolic possession, and He had at once exercised the authority that knew no bounds within all of creation. There is subtle divine anger in the prolonged scene which allows the demons to heap abuse upon themselves. The absurdity of the devil himself using the very form of exorcism and calling on the living God for protection against divine powers! Underlining this stupid clumsiness, Christ asked the exorcist's question: "What is thy name? And he saith to Him: My name is Legion, for we are many. And he besought Him much that He would not drive him away out of the country . . . saying: Send us into the swine, that we may enter into them" (Mark 5:9–10, 12). The Roman legion was a group of some five or six thousand men; the very thought of such a horde of demons must have held the disciples transfixed in horror. Christ recognized the answer as a mere ruse to avoid answering His question; but again, the picture of the proud champions of evil begging for admission to a herd of animals held to be unclean was not to be blurred but sharpened. He immediately gave permission, and going out of the man they entered into the herd of some two thousand swine; the madness of the man swept into the animals and the whole herd rushing into the sea were drowned. It is a sickening thought that the devils let loose in the world have their places of refuge, men and countries, where they are served, well received, even welcomed! Deprived of those ghastly homes, the demon faces the threat of a return to hell or, at the very least, the strong rebuff to such a graceless wanderer knocking at the door of the souls of men who know the joy of the presence of God.

Up to this moment, the poor victim had been completely passive. It was not his name that Christ sought; it was not he who answered, not he who pleaded against banishment at the word of Christ. He was still at the feet of Jesus. As the caretakers of the swine fled in terror to report the affair in the town, this poor creature was given clothes. When the owners of the swine came out to see for themselves what had happened, they found the former demoniac "sitting, clothed, and well in his wits, and they were afraid" (Mark 5:15). This was not a matter of a few wealthy men come to protest at the destruction of their property. Such a herd would represent the possession of most of the countryside, some owning only one, another as many as a dozen of the swine. It was, then, the whole people. They were afraid of Jesus, for they had seen for themselves what authority He exercised even over the demons; they wanted no trouble with Him, yet they wanted no contact with Him either. It was no source of joy to them that their countryside had been freed of such malicious power; they had got along well enough with the devil by keeping away from God, certainly they had never been forced to curb their illicit raising of the forbidden animals. They were polite, for they were afraid; yet they were coldly hostile, for their losses had been great. That a great benefit had been conferred on a miserable man meant nothing to them. Their demand was insistent that Christ depart from their coasts at once. It did not occur to them that it was not Jesus but the demons who had caused the swine to perish; He had done no more than give permission for their entry into the swine. If this represented a responsibility on His part, what a striking statement, from one with such authority, of the value of one man in the face of any material consideration! It was divine sovereignty going to extremes to shake men out of a condition of despair that drove them to embrace what should serve them because they admitted nothing worthy of their service.

The trip across the lake after a long day of preaching, the dangers of the storm, the entry into hostile country had, then, been for the sake of one single man; an outcast, utterly stripped of all things human and of any least regard from his fellowmen. A man abandoned by men; but well worth the special effort of the Son of God. This man of all that country knew what had been given to him. "And when He went up into the ship (for God is not an invader but a guest) he that had been troubled with the devil began to beseech Him that he might be with Him. And He admitted him not, but saith to him: Go into thy house to thy friends, and tell them how great things the Lord hath done for thee, and hath had mercy on thee. And he went his way, and began to publish in Decapolis how great things Jesus had done for him: and all men wondered" (Mark 5:18–20). Even these graceless people were not to be abandoned; they would be left cause for wonder, and wonder is often the wedge that can pierce open a closed mind.

In sharp contrast to the cold hostility of the pagans, a great multitude of Galileans gathered about Jesus on His return to their shores, and so quickly that, as Mark says, He was still "nigh unto the sea." Through that crowd, a certain Jairus, one of the principal men of a Capharnaum synagogue, made his way to the feet of Jesus, his path made easier both by the respect in which he was held and by the obvious desperation of his mission. The agony of anxiety that had brought him to Jesus left no room for careful preservation of dignity or for formally respectful address; throwing himself at the feet of Jesus, "he besought Him much, saying: My daughter is at the point of death; come, lay thy hand upon her, that she may be safe and may live" (Mark 5:23). Jesus knew well the difference between the tumbling words of anxiety and the stumbling words of lukewarm faith; here there was no challenge to the father's demands for His presence and the touch of His hand in benediction for the life of his child. Jesus set off immediately, "and a great multitude followed Him, and they thronged Him."

In the press of the crowd about Him was "a woman who was under an issue of blood twelve years, and had suffered many things from many physicians; and had spent all that she had, and was nothing the better, but rather worse." The vivid words are not a condemnation of the medical profession but a record of a still enduring, and still foolish, custom of the East; of calling in as many doctors as possible to diagnose and treat an ill member of the family. In fact, the number consulted was the gauge both of the affection of the family and of their affluence. Inevitably there would be differences of opinion and contradictory methods of treatment. It is not at all surprising that this woman was not better but rather worse. To understand the courage behind her approach to Jesus, it is not enough to see her discouragement at the long years of illness nor the personally disagreeable and embarrassing character of her disease; she was, by that illness, legally impure and rendered equally impure anyone who came in contact with her. She had either to approach Christ stealthily or make public confession of her embarrassment and immediately be driven in anger from the crowd for exposing them to legal impurity. Pressing through the crowd with something of the leper's disregard for the risks she ran, she came within reach of Jesus and, satisfied with the very minimum, touched the hem of His garment. "And forthwith the fountain of her blood was dried up, and she felt in her body that she was healed of the evil."

Jesus knew, through the divine enlightenment given His human mind, that a miracle had been worked through the instrumentality of His human nature; He would not know humanly who it was that had benefited by that miracle. Stopping and looking about on the crowd, He asked: "Who hath touched my garments?" To the disciples, the question seemed absurd, for of the thronging crowd any number might well have brushed against His garments. Only the woman knew the full import of that question; and it had been asked precisely for her benefit. She must not be allowed to go off in a superstitious belief that the touch of the garment had been the source of the miracle; she must know it came from her own faith and the beneficent will of Christ. "Fearing and trembling (she) came and fell down before Him, and told Him (and all the crowd) the truth. And He said to her: Daughter, thy faith hath made thee whole: go in peace, and be thou whole of thy disease" (Mark 5:33–34).

While the precious words were still falling on the ears of the grateful woman, messengers came from the house of Jairus with the news of his daughter's death; the idea of raising the dead was so far from their minds that they urged the grieving father not to bother Christ further.

It was, they thought, too late even for His power to accomplish anything. Jesus overheard the words, and reached out in instant sympathy to reassure Jairus: "Fear not, only believe." The word of the girl's death spread quickly through the crowd and made easy Our Lord's dismissal of them; if there were to be no miracle but only the fulfillment of the obligations of condolence, Jesus would have no difficulty in limiting His companions to Peter, James and John, the three disciples who were to be so favored in the great moments of what remained of His life. As this small group reached the house of mourning, they were met with the tumult of compassion which was the custom of the time and country; it was as yet too soon for the professional mourners to have been obtained, but the friends and neighbors who had watched at the bedside and helped about the house would immediately give the customary loud expression to their sympathy. "Going in, He saith to them: Why make you this ado, and weep? the damsel is not dead, but sleepeth." They knew better, indeed His question was in a way a reflection on them; in self-defense they gave the prompt answer of derision. Of course the girl was dead. Nevertheless, His words would serve to limit the publicity on the striking wonder He was about to work; though the memory of the widow's son would still be in their minds, men would need more time to ponder the parables before they were faced with more indisputable evidence that here indeed was the Messias. It would be easier for the mourners to admit a mistake on their part than to face the fact of the resurrection of one from the dead; on the other hand, the father, mother, and chosen disciples were witnesses enough to testify to the facts of the wonders of God's powers.

The dead girl still lay on the bed in which she had died. Looking down on her, Jesus saw a youngster of some twelve years, only a little younger than his own mother had been when she cradled Him in a manger in Bethlehem. Taking her dead hand in His own, Jesus said: "Damsel, I say to thee arise. And immediately the damsel rose up and walked" (Mark 5:41–42). In the Old Testament, the dead had risen through the instrumentality of Elias and Eliseus; but only after a terrific struggle of prayer and symbolic action, as if forcing the hand of God. Jesus spoke with authority, His own authority; there was not so much as a preliminary prayer in His banishment of death. Before death men are powerless and death invincible; the Son of God made man is master of the Sabbath and the sea, of health and disease, of devils and death. The few witnesses were astounded, for the naked power of God is not often seen by the eyes of men. Their stupefaction was so complete that the daughter for whom they had been so anxious and for whom they had so grieved was for the moment entirely forgotten. The thoughtfulness of Christ overlooked no smallest detail; it was He who "commanded that something should be given her to eat." He did not come among men for the purpose of stupefying them with miracles, rather He worked the miracles to awaken men and bring them to salvation. The least of men is a greater wonder than the greatest of miracles, for the kingdom of heaven is within him, and eternal life with God is within reach of the feeblest hand.

Leaving the house He had turned from one of mourning into one of joy, Jesus and His disciples continued on out of the city itself to take the road to Nazareth. It was a year now since He had left this place of His dearest memories, ending the long quiet years to undertake that for which He had come among men. At the end of this little journey, He would find His mother, Mary, in the home which could not be other than lonely, His closest kinsfolk, and the men and women with whom He had passed from infancy to manhood. Yet this was not a triumphant homecoming for a well-earned rest, the comfort of a loving welcome, and the pleasing applause of His townsfolk in honor of the great things they had heard of Him. He came to Nazareth to preach; there was, in fact, little welcome awaiting Him from anyone but His holy mother.

He stayed in Nazareth a few days; one of those days, the crucial one, was the Sabbath. Once, long months before, He had risen in that same little synagogue to read the Scriptures and announce the fulfillment of the prophecies in Him; then His reception had been kind, the people had been astonished and more than a little proud of His manner of preaching. The months had worked a disastrous change in the dispositions of the people of Nazareth. Pride had given way to jealousy as they heard of the wonders He worked and the sermons He preached in every part of Galilee, particularly in neighboring Capharnaum, while their own Nazareth got nothing but rumors and second-hand accounts.

Jealousy needs little or nothing of substantial fuel for its smouldering fires. By this Sabbath day when Jesus entered the synagogue, the people of Nazareth were well blinded to truth, and in no mood to give, nor to receive, mercy. Their astonishment at His words and works was quickly given a vicious twist of mockery. Others could gape at His wisdom, but they knew Him too well for that: He was the son of the widowed Mary, the carpenter; and when did carpenters find time for scrolls and wisdom's pursuit? They had watched His growth from infancy, where did this extraordinary power come from all of a sudden? Weren't they well acquainted with His cousins, kinsfolk so close as to be called brothers and sisters: James and Joseph, Jude and Simon? "And they were scandalized in regard of him" (Mark 6:3).

This was the first time in Jesus' experience that those so close to Him had turned so bitterly against Him, though it was not to be the last. The human hurt of it was deep; an outraged heart might easily have struck out in scorn and anger at such injustice. Yet Our Lord's answer was divinely patient. With deft words, He uncovered the cancer of jealousy that was eating at their souls: "Doubtless you will say to me this similitude: Physician, heal thyself; as great things as we have heard done in Capharnaum, do also here in thy own country. And He said: Amen I say to you, that no prophet is accepted in his own country" (Luke 4:23–24). In the face of such dispositions in men, there could be no question of favors from God. He recalled to their minds the prophets rejected by their fathers, and the strangers healed by those prophets. It was the undeniable truth of His diagnosis that fanned their smouldering jealousy into a raging conflagration of anger, and moved them to that violence which is anger's confession of defeat. They were in the synagogue and this was the Sabbath; yet they rose up, thrust Him out of the city to the brow of the hill "that they might cast Him down headlong. But He, passing through the midst of them, went His way" (Luke 4:29–30).

His mother, Mary, and the disciples were helpless witnesses of the jealousy, the anger, and the murderous violence turned loose on the one they loved so deeply. In later years, the remembrance of this rejection of the Master by His very own would be a source of persevering courage to the apostles as they met rejection, scorn, and violence on the roads of the world. For Mary, here and now, it was a terrifying and heart-breaking rehearsal for the tragedy of Calvary: the injustice, the blind anger, the mad rush of violence against the innocence and love of her Son. And she so helpless. On Calvary, He would have no recourse to His divine powers to escape the malice of men; nor is there any reason to suppose that it was supernatural power that accounted for His "passing through the midst" of the bloodthirsty citizens of Nazareth. Many a time since then a strong man, secure in his possession of himself, has met the uncontrolled violence of a cowardly mob with no weapon other than naked courage, and passed through the crowd to go his way unscathed.

Mary lived on in Nazareth, as she was to live on after Calvary, with little of comfort to lessen her share in the redemptive sufferings of her Son. The shame and remorse of burnt-out anger in their hearts would hardly make the people of Nazareth less vindictive towards Our Lady; in self-defense against the humiliation of their own guilt, they would strike again and again at innocence. Christ carried with Him a vivid remembrance of the ingratitude and injustice of the people among whom He had spent most of His days, and a divine insight into the continued sufferings of His mother, yet He did not swerve from His ministering pursuit of the little ones, the quest that had brought Him to Nazareth and now took him from there "through the villages round about teaching" (Mark 6:6).

9

GALILEAN CLIMAX

IT WAS during the winter that Jesus made His futile trip to Nazareth. It was the ideal time of the year to reach the little ones that Christ was seeking. The season has none of the rigors of our northern winters, but it does have the common note of leisure for men of the fields; there, however, the leisure is not forced by weather that makes farm work impossible, but rather it is taken as a natural reward for work well done. The fields have been sowed, and men sit back to wait for the harvest; they have time to talk, and a thirst for listening. Leaving Nazareth, Our Lord made the most of this opportunity: "And Jesus went about all the cities and towns, teaching in their synagogues, and preaching the gospel of the kingdom, and healing every disease, and every infirmity. And seeing the multitudes, He had compassion on them: because they were distressed, and lying like sheep that have no shepherd" (Matt. 9:35–36).

Our Lord's time in Galilee was growing short; the needs of these people could not be met by His personal efforts even if He did not take time either to eat or sleep. With the twelve He had so carefully chosen, sent out two by two, He could stir up to brightness the dimming fires that He had lit during this long year of ceaseless, uncounting labor. He had called them to be fishers of men; now the shortness of time moved Him to send them out for their first catch. By all human and divine standards, they would need much more preparation; indeed, before they would be scattered over the world, there would be the priceless human teaching and example of Christ up to the climax of Calvary and the divine outpouring of Pentecost to prepare their minds and their hearts fully. He called the twelve, and sent them forth on their first apostolic journey.

This was one of the finest moments in the life of the Son of Mary, one of the strongest, the most appealing to the rugged strength of men; the kind of moment in which a leader wins undying loyalty from men by the sheer nobility of his gesture. There was pity here, but a pity with iron in it, a pity which, for the sake of men, stripped Him of disciples and exposed both His work and His men to appalling risks. It asked the courage and faith of the apostles to do what He, who was God and man, had been doing: failure could plunge them into utter discouragement or even despair; success could ensnare them in the coils of pride; human respect could reduce them to compromise; the divine powers given them could sweep them into a tyrannous domination of men; either fear or pride could disrupt their loyalty to Him. Then, as now, Our Lord did not hesitate to impose risks on apostles where the souls of men were at stake. Still, there was thoughtfulness, too, for the men who were to carry such a burden. They were not yet ready to invade a foreign world where ignorance and hostility would go hand in hand; they were to work in a field which had already been plowed by Christ Himself, their preaching would be carefully confined to the limits of

Galilee, with Samaria and the Gentiles put aside for later efforts. What would pull the hearts out of the twelve in spontaneous loyalty was the sublime trust of Christ in the men He had chosen, the strong man's tribute to the strength of other men.

That challenging trust was evident in much more than the risks He asked them to take. They were to preach penance and announce the coming of the kingdom of God; a program that would demand the most of their hearers and be least welcome where it was most needed precisely because it there demanded the most. In confirmation of their preaching, they were to work the wonders that would leave men in no doubt that this was the world of God; for this, they were given lordly powers in a magnificent gesture of complete confidence: "Heal the sick, raise the dead, cleanse the lepers, cast out devils: freely have you received, freely give" (Matt. 10:8). They had indeed received freely, open-handedly; here was no niggardliness, no fear of rivals, no cautious hoarding of power by a weak or cowardly leader. The confidence of Christ in His men found equally strong expression in the challenging instructions He gave them for their apostolic labors. Summed up, those instructions demanded of the apostles a complete and voluntary poverty that was open dependence on the Providence of God, and such a total absence of self-interest as to win the immediate trust of men though it asked heroism of the apostles. They were not to take the precautions common to the least of travellers—some loaves of bread and a few coins hidden in girdle or headcloth for emergencies—much less indulge in the opulence of two coats. They must travel on foot, accoutered as a beggar but without the wallet the beggar ordinarily hoped to fill; not alone but in pairs, that they be witnesses, one to another, to uprightness of life and thereby preclude any slightest suspicion of wrongdoing; and with all of their time, all of their energy, devoted to the work of this apostolic mission. Arriving in a city, they must find a place suitable to the dignity of their message, depend on the hospitality of that home owner, and remain with him throughout their stay. Time was too short for social tours, souls were too important to risk the offense a change would give to the host, and their own comfort was in plain truth irrelevant. They were, above all, not to waste time. If a city gave them no hearing or one that stopped at the borders of curiosity, they were to shake the dust of that city off their sandals and be on their way in a relentless campaign for the souls of men. St. Mark adds a precious detail: "and they cast out many devils, and anointed with oil many that were sick, and healed them" (Mark 6:13). The Church has always recognized this as the preliminary of the sacrament of Extreme Unction, a religious, not a medical anointing, and so for the health of both body and soul; they had gone out, after all, as apostles not as medical doctors.

The challenging instructions of Christ sketched an authentic picture of the true apostle; and the work of that divine artist remains the pattern to which the apostle of any age must conform. These men of Christ, by His own demands, were driven men, men to whom time would always be much too short, the miles much too long, the strength in their bodies too frail a thing to do what had to be done; driven men who had behind them the conflagration of divine love, and before them the helpless misery of men urgently, desperately depending on the apostle's labors. He had gifts to give, and give abundantly; they had to be given quickly, to everyone, and a moment's dallying could mean eternal disaster for the individuals to whom he was sent. These men of Christ were poor men, so poor that no single possession could lay claim to their care. Poverty can be a bitter and dangerous thing, as much an occasion for theft and lying as riches can be for pride; but that is the poverty that is inflicted on a man, not the poverty that he embraces as a loyal friend. This latter kind of poverty is indispensable to the apostle. By it he is free for the work of God, free as a rich man can never be free of the entangling demands of his possessions; he is clearly unconcerned with material riches and men can see for themselves both that his concern for spiritual riches for them is sincere and that there is no taint of greed in the labors of his preaching; and he is, by his poverty, showing forth more brilliantly the power of God working through so lowly an instrument. Perhaps above all these advantages stands the almost necessary humility of the voluntarily poor; at least they will have, day after day, a diet of humiliation to make strong the sinews of humility. An apostle must be fed and clothed pretty much in conformity to the men of his time under penalty of defeating his work by embarrassing, amusing, or disgusting men; yet how can a man so poor as to have nothing live as other men? St. Thomas answers the difficulty in words that, for all the sanctity of the man, still have the flavor of humiliation in them: "A man may feed and clothe himself in conformity with others, not only by possessing riches, but also by accepting the necessaries of life from women and from those who are rich." Some men can be poor for the work of Christ because others who are rich are also generous. This was the food of humility insisted on by much more than Christ's mere words. "He chose all that was poor and despicable, all that was of small account and hidden from the majority, that we might recognize His divinity to have transformed the world. For this reason did He choose a poor little girl for His mother, a poorer fatherland; for this reason did He live as needy. Learn this from the manger."

It is at this moment that St. Mark looks back to tell the story of the martyrdom of John the Baptist. Herod, the ruler of Galilee, had of course heard of the miracles and teaching of Jesus long before this, but those reports and savored tales of miraculous works revolved around the personal efforts of Our Lord Himself; a kind of solitary wonder that need not be taken too seriously. But at this moment, with all of Galilee covered by the Lord Himself and His scattered apostles, the court of Herod was hit by a very flood of soundly authenticated tales of divine works done on all sides in the name of Jesus of Nazareth. The men of the countryside had time for talk at this season of the year, and they had more than enough to talk about; speculation about Jesus mounted by the hour, not less in the court of Herod than in the marketplaces of the Galilean cities. Some of the courtiers said: "It is Elias. But others said: It is a prophet, as one of the prophets" (Mark 6:15). From the dark depths of his uneasy soul, Herod's fear and guilt brought forth a terrifying identification: "John whom I beheaded, he is risen again from the dead" (Mark 6:16).

The story behind Herod's fear is a fusion of viciousness, weakness, silly vanity and ruthless pride; and in this it is not different from the usual story of men's great sins. Herod was weak rather than vicious, appreciative but half-fearful of great sanctity, and with no strong stomach for evil; more cautious than courageous, more prudent than bold, he could detest the thing he did, yet lack the strength to reject its doing. In his passion for his brother's wife, he had made enemies of his neighbors to the East by dismissing his wife, the daughter of their king; John's open accusation of adultery had threatened to alienate Herod's own people from him and thus isolate him from all loyalty of subject peoples. To his adulterous wife, John's accusation was more than a personal attack, the more deadly because of its undoubted truth; it threatened tragedy to this ambitious woman in its danger to Herod's throne. John had been promptly imprisoned. That was not enough for the vicious anger of Herodias, but it was the best she could get at the moment. John was protected from her in the prison; and Herod, recognizing sanctity and impressed by it almost to the point of enticement, heard the repeated admonitions of John, and heard him willingly. Knowing John, we know that his condemnation of the adulterous marriage did not soften. There could be nothing of comfort for the king in these interviews with John; on the other hand, Herodias would give him no peace in his toleration of John, for he was proving even more of a threat to her in prison. Herod could not keep away from John, yet neither could he dismiss Herodias. Her anger long since turned to bitter hatred, Herodias recognized her opportunity when Herod gathered the leading figures of his kingdom in the prison fortress of Machaerus for the celebration of his birthday. She knew what drink and lust will do to a man's reason; and Herod's only weapon of defense was his innate caution. When in her accurate judgment reason's barriers had been sufficiently battered down, she sent her daughter Salome to take the center of the stage from the professional dancing girls. The girl was of marriageable age for that time and country, about fifteen years old, with all the charm of youth's beauty made more appealing by the absence of the smooth hard surface of professional perfection in her dancing. Her royal blood gave added piquancy to lust; the obvious pleasure of his guests added fuel to the fires of the king's delight. "And he swore to her: Whatsocver thou shalt ask I will give thee, though it be the half of my kingdom" (Mark 6:23).

This was the moment for hatred's triumph; Herodias struck in defense of her debasement, and John had to die in defense of morality. The girl left the banquet hall, ostensibly to take counsel with her mother, a reasonable enough procedure if there had actually been any need of counsel. That there was no such need, and that Salome herself had been a full partner in the whole diabolical plan, is plain enough from the immediate decision of Herodias and the ready acquiescence of her daughter: not half of Herod's kingdom but the head of John the Baptist is to be the price exacted for the dance of a girl. Salome's consent, in the light of youth's infinite desires and the king's sweeping offer, needs the explanation of a maternal threat or promise, or of a hatred hardly less intense in the daughter than in the mother. At any rate, it is clear enough that hers was not a sullen subjection to maternal authority; she returned to the banquet hall "immediately and with haste to the king, she asked saying: 'I will that forthwith thou give me in a dish the head of John the Baptist' " (Mark 6:25). Herodias' counsel to Salome had been brutal enough to satisfy the almost insatiable vindictiveness of bitter hatred; but Salome could see in murder itself material for mocking pleasantry. It was her personal touch that demanded that the murdered man's head be served up in the banquet hall immediately, and on a platter! We are not told what happened to the appetites of the guests when this bloody morsel was paraded before them, nor is there any mention of what happened to the head of the martyr after it had been delivered into the vindictive hands of Herodias. We are told of the sadness of the weak king, the reluctance with which he fulfilled his oath and the cowardice that disregarded the sacredness of human life and the sanctity of the victim to escape the mockery of his companions at table and the displeasure of the girl. It is small wonder that now, long months after the death of the Baptist, Herod should see in Jesus his victim returned from the grave armed with supernatural power; the triumph of Herodias was a failure, for in fact the voice of John had not been silenced in the king's heart.

The apostles returned to Jesus from their apostolic mission as full of tales as sailors returned from the sea; and just as anxious to tell them all. They told Jesus all that they had done and had taught, the conclusion of each tale an occasion and an opportunity for the next and greater story. The scene is heart-filling in its humanness and we are drawn close indeed to those exultant men in our recognition of its human authenticity. Jesus' answer to the apostles' triumphant excitement is more divine than human. "And He said to them: 'Come apart into a desert place, and rest a little' " (Mark 6:31). As preachers making known divine truth, they could not hide from men in deserts but must necessarily walk and talk with the eyes of all men on them. They were emissaries sent to free men from their sins; it was not their office to sit waiting for men to come to them, but to walk all the highways and byways searching for the lost sheep, rushing on hurried feet as physicians of souls to those so desperately ill. They were to bring men to God.

That men might have easy access to these ambassadors of God, the apostles must live, as Christ lived, in an easy familiarity that would give confidence to the most timid. Still they were only men. It was for their instruction that the Lord Himself had found opportunity for solitary quiet even in the days when they had not so much as time to eat: a whole night of prayer on the mountain-top, the withdrawal alone or with a few again and again. As apostles, they simply could not stand an undivided public life of unceasing preaching. The exhaustion of the work obviously would call for physical rest. But over and above this, preachers of every age would need time for solitary prayer: time to refresh their souls, to renew the vigor of Christ which would drive them far beyond their own powers, time to restock the spiritual warehouse from which they were dispensing divine goods so unstintingly, time to ask for the indispensable divine help, and time to see their own littleness against the background of divine splendor. The apostle of every age needs hours of quiet, in a desert place, to escape the gratitude of men and the favors that flow from it lest he begin to work for that favor, to revel in that gratitude, to begin to suppose that both gratitude and favors are just rewards for personal excellence. At the very least, the apostle must have a corner in his heart as quiet and undisturbed as a desert, an inviolable cloister to which his mind and heart can retire for that intimacy with God which is rest for a man's soul.

The "desert place" chosen by Our Lord was a great plain just to the southeast of Bethsaida, a town on the east side of the Jordan river where it joins the Lake of Galilee. To reach it from Capharnaum, to which the apostles had returned, would demand only a very short boat trip across one little corner of the lake or a brief enough journey on foot around the northern end of the lake. When the little company set out by ship, people on shore could easily guess their destination, and a great multitude of them started on foot, for this time the Galilean crowd was not content to wait to receive Jesus, they followed Him. Leaving their ship, Jesus and His little company made their way over the green carpet of short-lived grass, spread even over this barren plain by the preceding rainy season, and climbed to a small plateau on the side of the mountain that runs all along this eastern shore. There Jesus sat down with His disciples gathered about Him to dispense some of that refreshment of soul to them. It was spring, for St. John tells us the feast of the Pasch was near (John 6:4). The setting was perfect for an apostle's restoration: the lovely clarity of a day in spring, the fresh young beauty of the land washed clean and invigorated by the rains, the serene quiet of the place, would all speak plainly of God; and there, in the very midst of the apostles, was God Himself talking to them.

It was not rest, however, that the apostles got; but only the sharply etched silhouette of its need and of its fitting circumstances. The following crowd soon caught up with them. Looking out over the very great multitude, Jesus had compassion on them and began to teach them many things. There is no breath of irritation, no slightest complaint in the gospel story at this total disruption of a well-earned rest; in the face of the needs of men, there is room only for compassion. The discourse of Christ continued until the uneasy disciples reminded Him both of the lateness of the hour and the barrenness of the place: "This is a desert place, and the hour is now past: Send them away, that going into the next villages and towns, they may buy themselves meat to eat" (Mark 6:35–36). Knowing well what He would do, Our Lord, in an almost playful aside, suggested to Philip that they should feed their guests; "and this He said to try him" (John 6:6). It would have been a fine opportunity for Philip, with the memory of Cana's miraculous nourishment in mind, to recognize the divine power and tender thoughtfulness of his Master; the moment, however, offered no spur to Philip's faith. His stunned mind reeled at the impossibility of such hospitality; to feed this enormous crowd would take a man's wages for two hundred days! With the simplicity of a child offering a penny to solve a million dollar debt, Andrew pointed out a young peddler who had five barley loaves, the bread of the poor, and two fishes; a futile help, as he himself recognized in asking the obvious question: "what are these among so many?" (John 6:9). With the provisions on hand, there would be one loaf of bread for each thousand men!

The impossibility of the situation merely marked out the limits of the efforts of men; Andrew would see for himself the answer to his question when divine power set to work. Jesus took charge as though He were host at a banquet; as indeed He was. Under His directions, the men were seated in companies of hundreds and fifties as guests would be assigned places around a dinner table. Then Jesus took the bread, gave thanks rather than blessed it, and distributed bread and fishes to the five thousand men. When they had eaten their fill, the fragments were gathered up as the crumbs would be after an ordinary Jewish meal; but of these fragments, there were twelve basketsful! "Now those men, when they had seen what a miracle Jesus had done, said: 'This is of a truth the prophet that is to come into the world.' Jesus therefore when He knew that they would come to take Him by force and make Him king, fled again into the mountain Himself alone" (John 6:14–15). These men could not miss the stupendous miracle that had been wrought; what they could not see as yet, though its outlines would soon begin to be made plain to them, was the parallel of this miraculous meal to the Eucharistic banquet whose definite promise would soon challenge the hearts of men.

The response of Jesus to the enthusiasm of the crowd had the same purpose as His patient teaching in the parables: the destruction of the cherished illusion of a Messias who would be a conqueror of Israel's enemies and king of this proud people. Our Lord was not a political revolutionary; He had not come to conquer nations but to save men. These men, above all, the apostles, must learn that His kingdom was not of this world, that His victory would not be over peoples but over sin. "He immediately obliged His disciples to go up into the ship" (Mark 6:45), that the apostles be no more seriously infected by the enthusiasm of the crowd. As for the crowd itself—well, it was already dusk; if He slipped away from them, they would soon be seeking shelter and by tomorrow their ardor would have cooled considerably.

The puzzled apostles, still much more men of their time than the other Christs they would some day be, reluctantly made their way to their ship. Jesus had said He would rejoin them, but it was already dusk and surely a little dallying would do no harm; He might come to them as soon as it was dark. When the dark settled and still He did not come, they set out to sea. They had covered a good deal of the short distance when they were met head on by one of the sudden storms common in spring, and the fury of the wind made their stoutest rowing efforts vain. The struggle between the rowing men and the wind-whipped waters was a stalemate for hours until inevitably their strength began to fail. About three o'clock in the morning, their astonished eyes gave them the message their minds could not accept: there was Jesus walking calmly on the stormy waters. Sailors see strange sights at sea, and in the dark of a stormy night, a man might well doubt he has seen anything, let alone such a sight as this: "and they, seeing Him walking upon the sea, were troubled, saying: 'It is an apparition.' And they cried out for fear. And immediately Jesus spoke to them, saying: 'Be of good heart: it is I, fear ye not' " (Matt. 14:26–27). Peter was not one to dally with doubts; bluntly, and with a sweeping assumption of his own courage, he challenged the dim figure on the sea: "Lord, if it be Thou, bid me come to Thee upon the waters" (Matt. 14:28). At the word of Jesus, Peter stepped boldly out of the boat and walked towards Jesus over the water. Unfortunately for his courage, he had a sailor's respectful knowledge of the fury of the sea; in that accurate estimation of the impossibility of his own position, his faith failed him. He began to sink; in his helplessness, his man's courage shrunk to a child's terror and "he cried out saying: 'Lord, save me.' And immediately Jesus stretching forth His hand took hold of him, and said to him: 'Thou of little faith, why didst thou doubt?' And when they were come up into the boat the wind ceased" (Matt. 6:30–32).

The journey continued without incident until they landed at Genesareth, somewhat south of Capharnaum; and immediately set out for that latter city. "And when they were gone out of the ship, immediately they knew Him: and running through that whole country, they began to carry about in beds those that were sick, where they heard He was. And whithersoever He entered, into towns or into villages or cities, they laid the sick in the streets, and besought Him that they might touch but the hem of His garment: and as many as touched Him were made whole" (Mark 6:54–56). He passed through a countryside of misery; and at His passing, mercy obliterated misery, the dark clouds of suffering were rolled away and bright sunshine lit up again the days of those who had almost forgotten joy. Miracles were scattered along the way in a reckless generosity that surpassed extravagance, as though, in a gesture of farewell to these people, the treasures of divine mercy were distributed in a final gesture of princely largesse. Jesus and His company made their way to the synagogue, for while it was not the Sabbath, that was the place for the vital discussion which was about to bring these Galilean days to their climax.

Meanwhile, the crowd left behind near Bethsaida had seen the apostles set sail without Jesus the evening before; and since boats never stayed on the eastern shore overnight, it was humanly impossible for Jesus to have completely escaped them. With the coming of morning, they searched for Him again, and soon satisfied themselves that wherever He was, He was not within their reach. There was nothing left for them to do but make their way on foot back to Capharnaum. Some of the more enthusiastic of the king-makers among them, those who had been the leaders in the movement of the night before, saw with joy that there were some ships approaching from Tiberias to Bethsaida. They immediately took advantage of this chance for speedy return and boarded ship for Capharnaum, their determination to realize the long cherished dreams of a kingly Messias still warming their hearts and hurrying their feet.

They found Jesus in the synagogue at Capharnaum;

they were delighted but still mystified as to the manner of His return from Bethsaida, and it was bewilderment that crowded to the fore in their greeting of Him: "Rabbi, when camest Thou hither?" (John 6:25). A direct answer would necessarily have included an account of the miraculous walking on the stormy waters and the divine calming of the sea; while Jesus had just scattered miracles with a generous hand among the folk whose misery focused their eyes on their own suffering, these questioners would make of further wonders fuel for the fires of their ambitions for an earthly king and a kingdom of abundance. Instead of answering their question, Jesus shaped the issue that now had to be settled once and for all by making plain to them the real reason for their enthusiasm: "You seek Me, not because you have seen miracles, but because you did eat of the loaves, and were filled" (John 6:26).

The old illusion of a royal Messias still endured; they were enthusiastic at the prospect of effortless abundance to be given them by the conqueror of their enemies. "Labor not for the meat which perisheth, but for that which endureth unto life everlasting, which the Son of man will give you. For him hath God the Father sealed" (John 6:27). It is a spiritual, not an earthly kingdom, that the Messias establishes; the old error must be corrected with no mincing of words, flatly, openly, whatever the cost. To this end, Jesus launched into a discourse on the sublime and mystical doctrine of the Bread of Life.

A whole year of His short public life had already been consumed by Jesus in teaching the people of Galilee; there was no time, now, for gentle, delicate preparation of their minds and hearts. Looking back over that busy year, He had preached penance to them; He had worked miracles on a grand scale to confirm His teaching, to manifest His divine power, to entice them with the divine goodness. He had shown beyond doubt His authority over the minds of men, over their sins, and over the Sabbath day. He had proclaimed Himself a lawgiver perfecting the Old Law by His new dispensation. Even the dullest of men would by this time have begun to think of Him as the Messias and to look to the kingdom the Messias would establish and secure. Unless men could be made to abandon the false hope of an earthly kingdom and see clearly the kind of spiritual kingdom in the hearts of men that Jesus had come to found, the labors of the Lord would be in vain and the hopes of men would be doomed to bitter disappointment. Obviously, the gentle approach by way of parables had not succeeded in dissipating the old, false dream. This was the crucial moment of the whole ministry in Galilee: failure could come about now either through His disciples continuing in their misunderstanding of His kingdom and so following a false light to their doom; or they could see clearly the nature of that kingdom, refuse to accept it, and abandon Jesus. This was the moment of decision, a moment that brought out the strong courage of Christ in sharpest relief.

This group to whom He was speaking was a friendly, even an enthusiastic crowd. Starting from their enchantment with the miraculous loaves He had given them, Christ turned their minds to a spiritual bread, a nourishment enduring to everlasting life to be had from Him whose words and works had so often been thoroughly authenticated by the power of God in miracles. The willingness of His audience found expression in their answer: "What shall we do that we may work the works of God?" They were thinking, naturally enough, in terms of external works, of fulfillment of a law by an observance that could be checked off step by step; what Jesus was asking them for at this moment was not external deeds but faith, a faith so sweeping and complete as to astound His hearers. "This is the work of God, that you believe in Him Whom He hath sent." They understood His demand clearly enough; in their eyes, all the wonderful things He had done were not evidence enough to support a demand for so total a submission of the minds of men. He was putting Himself up higher than Moses, and some special sign of God would be necessary to win the acquiescence of men; Moses had given them manna in the desert, bread from heaven, what comparable sign did He offer? Meeting the challenge, rather than taking offense at it, Our Lord answered that Moses had not given them heavenly bread; the bread of God is the bread that comes down from heaven and gives life to all the world, not merely the sustenance of life for this individual. It is this bread He offers them. Not unfriendly, but still thinking in terms of earthly abundance, the crowd answers: "Lord, give us always this bread." They had not yet followed Christ to the heights to which all His words invited them, they were still not facing the ultimate decision that must be made between the earthly and the spiritual kingdom; in plain words Jesus laid out before their minds the truth of Himself and of His demand for their faith: "I am the bread of life: he that cometh to Me shall not hunger; and he that believeth Me shall never thirst." He Himself is the bread come down from heaven, a spiritual bread that need not be given again and again, but that endures to life everlasting; but to have it, they must come to Him, must believe in Him.

Looking into their hearts, Our Lord saw with distress how disturbed they were. They had looked for promises of victory, for present glory, and the good things that belong to conquerors; instead, they had heard no word of such comfort but rather references to everlasting life, the last day, spiritual life to the world. Their disappointment was profound; already in their hearts they were deserting this disappointing Messias. In quick pity, Jesus reached out to them with kindly explanations, in words that are almost a plea. He will reject none of them who come to Him, none of those who, drawn by the Father, will believe in Him; He will lose none of them, and will raise them up to everlasting life. It is men who will reject Him, not He Who will reject men; and they have, in fact, already done so: "But I say unto you, you also have seen Me and you believe not."

The crowd, meanwhile, had been swelled by the arrival of open enemies of Jesus; the Scribes and Pharisees whom St. John consistently calls the Jews. They had had no difficulty in following the full meaning of the words of Our Lord; they had not missed the significance of one sent by the Father, coming down from heaven, giving life to the world. In cold enmity they muttered refutations of such a claim: "Is not this Jesus, the son of Joseph, whose father and mother we know? How then saith he, I came down from heaven?" Jesus met this deliberate hostility as a strong man would, impatient of subterfuge, bringing the point at issue sharply into the open, and then joining battle with no thought of compromise or surrender. Reading their hearts, He scorned the sly secrecy of their murmurings and sharply challenged their assumption of judicial power; they were, in fact, the very last ones in a position to pass judgment here, the very ones who could not teach because they had not been taught of the Father, they had rather trusted in their own learning than been drawn by God. They could not come to Him and still maintain their proud self-sufficiency. "Every one that hath heard of the Father, and hath learned, cometh to Me. Not that any man hath seen the Father; but He Who is of God, He hath seen the Father" (John 6:45–46). This was staggeringly clear to these learned men: here was One Who was of God, Who sees God; Who is this but the very Son of God?

Brushing aside all further quibbling, Jesus makes a flat statement of the sublime mystery of His own person, and of the unconditioned faith that men must bring to that mystery. "Amen, amen I say unto you: He that believeth in Me, hath everlasting life. I am the bread of life. Your fathers did eat manna in the desert, and are dead. This is the bread which cometh down from heaven; that if any man eat of it, he may not die. I am the living bread which came down from heaven. If any man eat of this bread, he shall live forever; and the bread that I will give, is my flesh, for the life of the world" (John 6:47–52). The reward of such faith is life everlasting; as for Christ Himself, He is bread from heaven, living bread, a bread eaten for immortality, that bread is His flesh for the life of the world! The words of the Lord were received with astonishment by all His hearers. The friendlier ones no doubt tried to still the protests within themselves by some kind of figurative or metaphorical interpretation of His words; His enemies scoffed at the words as absurd, intolerable, "How can this man give us His flesh to eat?" To neither group does the Lord make any least concession; this is the truth, not to be watered down in the name of cowardice. With all the splendid energy of His great soul and the full authority of His sublime person "Jesus said to them: 'Amen, amen I say unto you: Except you eat the flesh of the Son of man, and drink His blood, you shall not have life in you. He that eateth my flesh, and drinketh my blood, hath everlasting life: and I will raise him up in the last day. For my flesh is meat indeed: and my blood is drink indeed. He that eateth my flesh, and drinketh my blood, abideth in me, and I in him. As the living Father hath sent me, and I live by the Father: so he that eateth me, the same also shall live by me. This is the bread that came down from heaven. Not as your fathers did eat manna, and are dead. He that eateth this bread, shall live forever" (John 6:54–59).

At these words, all debate ended. Their clarity left no room for argument. The enemies of Christ were more than content with the literal acceptance of His words, and the effect of that acceptance on those who had been following Christ; clearly, it gave them a victory they could not have obtained by arguments of their own. Bewildered, beyond their depth, the weaker of the disciples who had held no more than a wavering loyalty to Christ, who were indeed by this time only nominally His followers, now broke off even that feeble bond; but others, men who had loved Him and followed Him with great loyalty, were saddened at these "hard" sayings, and turned away from Him in their hearts. It was to these last that the mercy of Jesus made one last appeal: He offered the miracle of reading their hearts to bolster their shaken faith; and held out to them the promise of the great sign of the Ascension as a confirmation of His descent from heaven to live among men; He coaxed them with the assurance that much more than mere flesh was necessary for the salvation of men, for even the flesh of God would avail men nothing if they did not eat it spiritually; that is, in the dispositions of grace becoming to a son of God. He asked for their patient trust. But it was all in vain. "After this many of His disciples went back; and walked no more with Him."

Jesus watched them go and in their going, saw the crumbling failure of His year of mercy, power, and truth in Galilee. Later, He would watch His apostles flee for their lives, leaving Him alone in the Garden surrounded by His enemies; still later, He would hang alone on a cross and watch all the world as it howled for His death. The rejection of God by men is a sad, sad sight, even for the myopic eyes of men; the eyes of God alone can see the full bitterness of this sad sight. Yet here, in this city by the sea, the deserting disciples could so easily have been won back to Him. He would only have had to say a word of explanation to put their minds at ease, no more than the easy assurance that His words were not to be taken literally, that He was speaking only in metaphors, that of course men were not to live by the flesh and blood of the Son of man. He had, in other words, only to compromise the truth, only to deny the sublimity of the mystery, only to lie the least bit; but then, on the same condition, He could have escaped the Cross. He had come that men might have the truth and the truth might make them free; the execution of such a mission leaves no room for compromise.

So many of His disciples found this mystery intolerable that Jesus, looking about as they left Him, found Himself so nearly alone that He could turn to the chosen twelve as the last remnants of the hosts that had followed Him. How long ago was it that He had fed five thousand? Even so, the issue of truth was paramount, the spiritual nature of His kingdom must be acknowledged, the faith men would give Him must be complete, unquestioning; not even to ease His aching human heart would He hold to this little group under any lesser conditions. "Then Jesus said to the twelve: 'Will you also go away?' " Peter, answering for the twelve, spoke with the unassailable logic of a man faced with a choice between the impenetrable mystery of God and the chaotic contradiction of nothingness: "Lord, to whom shall we go? Thou hast the words of eternal life. And we have believed, and have known, that Thou art the Christ, the Son of God." Peter spoke from his unwavering faith, and thereby gave Christ precisely what He had demanded of men; Peter did not pretend to scale the heights of the Lord's sublime teaching here, he did not ask that things be made plain to him, it was enough that he had the words of Jesus Christ to guide him through the darkness of things too bright for human eyes.

The answer of Peter and the loyalty of the apostles were a sadly needed comfort to Our Lord in this moment of failure. Yet even in that comfort there was a hard knot of bitterness: "Jesus answered them: 'Have not I chosen you twelve; and one of you is a devil?' Now He meant Judas Iscariot, the son of Simon: for this same was about to betray Him, whereas he was one of the twelve." The ministry in Galilee had failed; the Galileans had refused to understand what kind of Messias He is. All the mercy, power, and truth of God had failed to eradicate the deadly dream of revenge, conquest, earthly abundance. From now on, Jesus and His little band would walk the roads outside of Galilee as the Lord prepared the apostles for the tragedy of Calvary, the glory of the resurrection, and the continuation of His life in the Church even to the end of time.

10

A TIME APART

THE first year of Our Lord's ministry seems fully accounted for by His labors within Galilee. As far as the Evangelists tell us, He went up to Jerusalem only once during that year, in the spring for the feast of the Pasch; for the rest, working out of Capharnaum as a headquarters, He plowed every inch of Galilee, harrowed it, scattered the seed of God with an extravagant hand, soaked it with a rain of miracles numerous beyond men's concept of generosity, while the sunshine of His merciful goodness penetrated to the very marrow of the land. Yet the harvest was so pitifully small that He could make a full reckoning of it in one quick glance at this faithful band. God does not take the heart of a man by storm, men are not forced into heaven, no man is saved against his will; this awful truth, of God's complete reverence for man's free will and man's terrible responsibility for his own soul, echoes from the life of Christ like a thunderclap blanketing the centuries with a smashing sound that shrinks the excuses of men to frightened whispers. If ever a land was favored of God, it was Galilee; yet all the truth of God, the power of God, His eager mercy and patient understanding, did not win Him an entry into the hearts of men.

This second year of Our Lord's ministry was spent on the road. The Evangelists trace His steps to the west, to the north, to the east, to the south: to Tyre and Sidon, to Caesarea Philippi, to Perea, to Judaea, and Jerusalem; and throughout the year there are lightning thrusts into and withdrawals from Galilee, like tantalizing flicks of a rapier, searching out some weak spot in men's perverse defense against God. This year finds Him invading Jerusalem's stronghold of hostility in the early summer for the feast of Pentecost, in the early fall for the feast of Tabernacles, and in mid-winter for the feast of Dedication. But in each case, He is in and out before hate can muster its murderous forces. There is no question this year of a headquarters, of a city that can be called His own; He and His apostles move through these days with all the unpredictable agility of a task force at sea.

The difference in this second year's ministry is much greater than a mere matter of mobility. Clearly, it held out no possibility of a sustained preaching campaign nor any prospect of a gradual enlightenment by patient teaching of an unchanging audience. What the men of Galilee lost, the apostles gained. They had Christ much more to themselves; inevitably the bonds of friendship would grow stronger from the more constant physical companionship, the threats, the danger, the general air of maneuver, but above all from so many long, quiet hours on the road, and in the still of the evening. From the gospel story, it is clear that this whole year was divinely designed for a purpose altogether distinct from the year in Galilee; this was a time set apart for the chosen twelve. All the wisdom of the Word of God made man now focused on their formation; the contacts with men were hardly more than interruptions, usually quick brushes with the enemy, which themselves were made to serve the purpose of preparing the apostles for the years and the centuries after the Master's death. Our Lord, after the excessive gift of a third of His public life to Galilee, was busy now building His Church, extending His life to the little ones of all the centuries. His gift of truth in this second year is deeper, subtler, more divinely transcendent as it concentrates more on the mystery of Christ Himself, His person, His sacrifices, the divine demands to be made on His followers.

After the wholesale desertions of Galilee, Jesus and the twelve took the road to Jerusalem, merging with the pilgrims going up to that city for the feast of Pentecost. In the seven weeks since the feast of the Pasch, the fields had ripened, and now was the time to offer the first fruits of the harvest to the Lord; the contrast between the harvest given Christ by men, and that given men by God is its own commentary. We know nothing of that journey to Jerusalem, but come upon Jesus standing, unrecognized, in the midst of the multitude of sick, blind, lame, withered men crowding the five colonnades of the healing pool of Bethsaida (John 5:2). The pool held slim hopes of relief since the movement of the waters, which was the sign of its curative action, promised a cure only to the first to enter the waters thereafter. Jesus singled out a man who had held to that slim hope for years and years and asked him: "Wilt thou be made whole?" The question could easily have been resented as foolish; but not when asked by Our Lord, and not by one so naively simple as this helpless sick man. His answer was rather a statement of how earnestly he had hoped and how helpless he was since he could not get himself into the water; indeed this may have been the precise purpose of the question of Christ, to bring sharply to the man's mind the seeming hopelessness of a cure. Obviously, the possibility of a miracle had not occurred to the sick man, nor did he look to Christ for any immediate relief. "Jesus saith to him: Arise, take up thy bed, and walk. And immediately the man was made whole." Jesus slipped off into the crowd unnoticed, His one merciful purpose for coming here accomplished. Apparently no one had listened to the interchange between Our Lord and the sick man, no one had witnessed the miracle. But the sudden activity of the sick man, his joyous declaration of the wonderful thing that had happened to him while he went about gathering up his possessions, spread the story of the miracle in no time at all. He had, indeed, not moved away from the portico carrying the mat which was his bed, before he was challenged sharply by the Pharisees and doctors of the law; for this was the Sabbath day. There is a revealing contrast in the response of the cured man and the questions of the enemies of Christ: to this good man, it seemed more than sufficient that the one who had cured him had told him to take up his bed; while the Pharisees, uninterested in the miracle-worker, sought the name of the breaker of the Sabbath. But Jesus had come and gone so quietly, the cured man could give them no information.

We do not know whether or not the man ever did get his bed home with him that Sabbath day; but he did get to the Temple to give thanks to God for the favor he had received. There, as if by chance, Jesus found him for the double purpose of making Himself known and of warning the man not to use his restored health, as many another has done through the ages, to sin against the God who had given it to him. Without malice, sure in his simplicity that gratitude would flood the hearts of all men as it did his, he told the Scribes and Pharisees that it was Jesus who had cured him of his illness.

It was almost immediately after His arrival in Jerusalem then, that Jesus was thrown into open and radical conflict with these leaders of the people. "Therefore did the Jews persecute Jesus, because He did these things on the Sabbath" (John 5:16). As a matter of fact, the order to the sick man did not violate the Law, but it did run counter to the man-made regulations to which these leaders tried to give the full force of the Law. The Sabbath was a day of rest, imaging and commemorating the rest of God after the six days of creation. None of the learned men of the Jews supposed for an instant that God had ceased to work in the world and in Israel when creation was completed; obviously His rest was not an absolute cessation from activity, nor was the rest of the Sabbath meant to be any more so. The carrying of burdens outside the walls, that is for commercial transactions, was forbidden; and this Jesus faithfully observed. His answer to the persecutors probed the abscess of their error, but the pain of it went unnoticed in their outrage at the content of His answer: "But Jesus answered them: My Father worketh until now; and I work. Hereupon therefore the Jews sought the more to kill Him, because He did not only break the Sabbath, but also said God was His father, making Himself equal to God" (John 5:17–18).

The Jews had understood Him rightly. He was not abrogating the Sabbath but claiming His mastery of it on extraordinary grounds: the right of the Son to act as the Father does, and the Son's intention to exercise that right. The words He used precluded anything but the strictest literal sense of His words; He was not calling Himself a son of God in the sense that any just man is a son of God, He was stating flatly the unity of nature that was His and the Father's. His answer was profound, rich in breathless implications; and it was rightly understood. If He were no more than a man, He was indeed a blasphemer; and the penalty of such blasphemy was death. Here was a man making Himself equal to God, one in nature with the Father.

In the eyes of His apostles, Jesus must have taken on gigantic stature as His great heart met these challenges without the slightest wavering. In Galilee so recently, He had suffered the triumph of His enemies and the almost total desertion of His followers rather than deny that it was by eating His flesh and drinking His blood that men would have life in them. Here He faced murderous rage and a determined threat to His life. But here, as in Galilee, it would have been so easy for cowardice to escape the crisis. Our Lord had only to speak a word against the truth and the hostility would have evaporated. Let Him say that He had been speaking in metaphors, that He was not really God's eternal Son, that He was merely claiming the title that any just man can rightly claim without any pretension to divinity, and there would be no grounds for thoughts of murder in the minds of His enemies. In Galilee, the truth had cost him His friends; in Jerusalem, it was clear that the truth might easily cost Him His life. The course He chose was to leave absolutely no doubt in the minds of men about the truth with which He had come to free men.

His answer to the rage of His enemies was to make a clear statement of His right to speak and to act as He does, the right of the incarnate Son of God; to draw out in all their shocking details the consequences of His divinity; and to fire proofs of these sublime claims at His enemies at point-blank range. He does not ask them to deny the humanity that is so evidently His, but He insists on the divinity that is united to that humanity in His divine person. From the human nature He took from His mother Mary, comes the fullness of subjection, of dependence, of reverence that is due the divine Father from every man; from the divine nature that is His by the eternal generation from the everlasting Father, comes the absolute equality of power, of knowledge, of life with that divine Father. It is not merely as the eternal Son of God that He speaks, but as the Son of God made man through the sinless virgin. So He can do nothing of Himself, as man, but what He sees the Father doing. But He does see *all* things that the Father does; the Father shows Him all things in an abandon of love that is infinite, that knows no keeping of secrets. What the Father does He does also, and in the same manner. Though their consequence will be the disappointing one of stupefaction rather than faith, the Father will show still greater works than the miracles that have already been done, and the Son will do these greater works: such great works, for example, as the gift of life and the absolute justice of irrevocable judgment.

Lest there be any slightest grounds for mistake, let the consequences be clearly stated. Equal honor is due to Father and Son: "that all men may honor the Son as they honor the Father. He who honoreth not the Son, honoreth not the Father, who hath sent him" (John 5:23). Life everlasting is had by belief in Christ, and so in the Father. Indeed, those who so believe will not come to judgment as men accused, but pass from death to life. Life belongs to God, all others merely share it; "As the Father hath life in Himself, so He hath given to the Son also to have life in Himself." That gift of life is already being given that men dead in their sins might come to the life of grace: "Amen, amen I say unto you, that the hour cometh, and now is, when the dead shall hear the voice of the Son of God, and they that hear shall live." The work of judgment, the work that only God can possibly do for only God knows the hearts of men, is given to the Son who is also man, that men be judged both humanly and divinely beyond all grounds for resentment of that judgment. Beyond the present spiritual resurrection of the sinners, there awaits the physical resurrection which will bring all men, body and soul, to judgment, and that too will come at the voice of the Son: "for the hour cometh wherein all that are in the graves shall hear the voice of the Son of God."

Here again were "hard sayings," bitterly hard for the men who cherished the dream of a conquering Messias and the abundance flowing so easily from His earthly conquests; doubly bitter for the proud leaders who smashed their arguments against the truth of God. Christ, reading their hearts, could see them marshalling the obvious defense against His divine words: this man makes statements with no proofs; why should anyone accept claims that are no more than His own witness to Himself? If it is proofs they want, He answers, there are proofs aplenty; and on grounds that they themselves revere. They had not championed the Baptist in his lifetime, but now that he was dead, a martyr to the moral law, even these former enemies held him in esteem: "You sent to John, and he gave testimony to the truth" —he did indeed testify to the Lamb of God. But this, being human testimony, is the least of the proofs; one offered only from the compassionate heart of the Christ they were harrying: "But I receive not testimony from man: but I say these things, that you may be saved."

There is a much greater witness to the divine authenticity of Christ's words, the works themselves which cried aloud from the days of this past year like the voice of God, divine works, miracles that only God could work: the sight given to the blind, the life given to the dead, the instantaneous health that shattered the reign of sickness as light annihilates darkness. If the Father's testimony in the miraculous works be not enough, there is the direct testimony of His words in the Sacred Scriptures which these leaders of the nation study so diligently and hold in such high reverence. "(You) search the Scriptures, for you think in them to have life everlasting; and the same are they that give testimony of me." Yet this testimony is refused, and on what grounds? They have never heard God's voice, have never seen His face even as dimly as did the patriarchs who were their fathers; moreover, they never held the word of God in their hearts. How can they accept the word of God in testimony to His Son? As a matter of fact, they approached the Scriptures, not as an object of faith, but as a subject of study; and it was the study, not the living acceptance, of the Scriptures that was in their eyes the holy work par excellence. They came to the word of God without humble hearts, and sought in that word some promise of a Messias who would be a divine instrument to impose their caricature of the Law on the whole world. Actually, the Scriptures give testimony to a Messias who should be listened to, from whom they should learn, who spoke with authority because He was the Son of God. It is in Him, not in the Scriptures, that life is found. There is profound sadness in Christ's conclusion of His argument: "and you will not come to me that you may have life."

In all His conflicts with the Scribes and Pharisees,

Jesus is never the helpless quarry, driven to bay by relentless pursuers, and finally overwhelmed by sheer numbers. It is not He who suffers defeat, but again and again it is the leaders of the Jews who are reduced to confusion and by the very weapons they themselves have selected for the battle with Christ. If we remember that the souls of these men were beyond price in His eyes, we can understand His patient human argumentation, the while He holds in leash the lightning of divine wisdom and divine power. When that merciful patience has confounded their arguments, yet left their hostility undiminished, it is that same earnest love of them which launches into terrible attack in the hope of shattering their pride and shaking them awake to their own souls' salvation. So it was here. Christ had gone to great lengths to prove He was no glory-seeker sounding His own trumpet; now He says it plainly, and attacks in words that should have struck terror to their hearts. "I receive not glory from men. But I know you, that you have not the love of God in you."

The accusation was devastating to men whose whole lives were dedicated to the Law and the Temple. Christ offers no argument in its support beyond the indubitable testimony of the guilty consciences so naked to His divine knowledge. Without the love of God in their hearts, they are badly disposed to God and to Moses in whom they trust; they cannot recognize one whom God has sent, for pride has eaten the heart out of their love and left it a dead thing. They are not the defenders of God's glory, it is not for them to sit in judgment on blasphemy, God's honor has not been committed to their care. Christ came in the name of His Father, and they will not receive Him; yet others will come, in their own name, doing no divine works, and they will be championed by these very Scribes and Pharisees. This prophecy of Christ was abundantly fulfilled in the very lifetime of those who listened to Him. In a final gesture of mercy, the greater for its very sternness, Jesus uncovered for them the root of their stubborn resistance to God. They had fallen into the special trap pride readies for the feet of learned men: the vanity of mutual admiration, of learned recognition, that so easily becomes the lifeblood of men of books. It was not Christ but His enemies who were the glory-seekers. They had no greater joy than the citation of an opinion of theirs by other doctors; the approval or disapproval of the ordinary people was a matter of disdain to them, but the absence of learned recognition was catastrophic. It was not glory from God that they sought, a glory that might well be enveloped in silence and obscurity, but the plaudits of their own specialized group. "How can you believe, who receive glory one from another: and the glory which is from God alone you do not seek?"

However, Our Lord will not descend to the position of their accuser; He is their judge. The accusation will be taken care of by Moses; they have taken his words as material for endless exegesis, but turned their back on the preparations made in the Scriptures for the future and the Messias who would fulfill the prophecies and perfect the Law. "Think not that I will accuse you to the Father. There is one that accuseth you, Moses, in whom you trust. For if you did believe Moses, you would perhaps believe me also; for he wrote of me. But if you do not believe his writings, how will you believe my words?" They had substituted study for belief and built up pride's impenetrable walls for their own imprisonment.

"After these things Jesus walked in Galilee; for He

would not walk in Judaea, because the Jews sought to kill Him" (John 7:1). The stay in Jerusalem had been short indeed, but momentous: only long enough to cure a man who had hoped beyond all of hope's limits, and to wage one sharp battle with the Scribes and Pharisees; yet momentous enough to lay bare the loveless pride that cut these leaders off from God and to sketch in firmer, clearer lines still more of the details of the mysterious truth of God made man. After that brief sally into Jerusalem, Christ and the apostles took the road to Galilee; it was not yet time to meet the full force of the hatred of men in the supreme defense of truth. The pattern of a brief encounter and quick withdrawal will occur again and again this year; not always to escape hostility, but always with the precious consequence of time alone. We have no account at all of that three or four day journey from Jerusalem to Galilee, nothing of the words that fell from the lips of Christ, the questions asked and the answers given as the road passed under their feet, as they sought shelter from the sun at noonday, as they came to a halt in the peace of the evening; no details of the prayer which prepared for sleep's imitation of death and followed from the wonder of sunrise and awakening. These things were not written into the books but on the hearts of the apostles.

We find Jesus, the hidden journey accomplished, in Capharnaum. St. Mark's account lets us know that the authorities in Jerusalem did not underestimate the danger Jesus posed to their high position and their empty doctrines; they had sent some of the Scribes from there to Capharnaum, for this man was to be hunted down remorselessly. As the scene unfolds, we see Our Lord interrupting His teaching of the crowd to withdraw with His apostles, so that they might eat a little. The

Pharisees of Galilee, also on hand despite their earlier triumph in the desertion of the disciples a few months previously, joined forces with the Scribes from Jerusalem, for even without disciples this man shattered their hopes of a worldly Messias, overthrew their cluttering of the law, and saw too clearly the depth of their pride. Watching the Lord and His apostles while they ate, they quickly found the opening they hoped for; the apostles took their food without the ritualistic washing of the fingers. "Why," they asked Christ, "do not thy disciples walk according to the tradition of the ancients, but they eat bread with common hands?" (Mark 7:5). There was no question here of the Law, for not even these doctors attempted to find a basis in law for the obligation they imposed, but contented themselves with the authority of the tradition of the ancients; nevertheless, St. Mark is accurate in describing the great mass of the people, dominated by the Scribes and Pharisees, as bowing to their word and striving for the prescribed legal purity of food, of person, and of utensils. There was no question here of physical cleanliness, but of a legal purity which had a general observance, though, of course, there were varying degrees of carefulness in the observance. Here then was the challenge to Christ: through your disciples you do what is forbidden.

They stood, smugly confident of the solidity of their accusation, prepared to meet the wrigglings and evasions that their experience in debate led them to expect. They should have known better than to expect evasions from Christ; but even a graphic memory of those previous conflicts with the Lord could not have prepared them for His answer. Perhaps it was because, being a little apart from the crowd, He could more easily let mercy's sternness go its full length, perhaps it was because this time the enemies had attacked not Him but his disciples; whatever the reason, His answer was a scathing blast that left them gaping and dismayed: "Well did Isaias prophesy of you hypocrites, as it is written: This people honoureth me with their lips, but their heart is far from me. And in vain do they worship me, teaching doctrines and precepts of men. For leaving the commandment of God, you hold the tradition of men. . . . Well do you make void the commandment of God that you may keep your own tradition." With a gesture impatient of pettiness, He had brushed aside their question to launch a smashing attack on the very principle of their rabbinical tradition, to storm with no counting of the cost at the very citadel of the power and pride of the Scribes and Pharisees. They were hypocrites in the exact meaning of the words of the great prophet, their piety a thing of sheer pretense. It was not only that they burdened men with futile precepts, they went to the lengths of voiding the law of God, abandoning the divine law for the traditions of men.

These were violent words, damning words; yet they were not the extravagant fumings of a man beside himself with anger, but the calculated charges of a strong man's disgust for the cowardice of deceit and hypocrisy, of a holy man's clear vision of the catastrophe wrought on men by leaders who abandon God. Nevertheless, such charges cannot be hurled in the teeth of men without substantiation. Christ proved His accusation beyond all quibbling by citing one undeniable example of the annulment of the natural law with its immediate source in the eternal law of God by these very traditions for which the Scribes and Pharisees demanded respect. By taking a vow a man could consecrate a thing to God and thereby withdraw it from all profane, that is non-sacred use, except his own; thus, to avoid the natural obligation to feed or clothe indigent parents, a son could, and did, take such a vow which immediately and for all time forbade his sharing his goods with his parents. The practice of this nefarious trickery was a fact; it may have been a worry to this or that rabbi, but he would defend such an immoral vow because of the tradition of the ancients. That tradition insisted that a promise to God was binding, was a vow; in actual fact, such a promise was an insult to divinity. A vow is a serious promise to God of a better good; an immoral vow is no vow at all. Yet these men insisted on the observance of the immoral vow to the annulment of the divine law. This was not an isolated case: "many other such like things you do." Our Lord had not deigned to answer the question put to Him by the doctors; instead, He had cast serious doubt on the whole pharisaic tradition which made obligatory things that were violations of the law of God.

This was enough of an answer; let the Pharisees themselves judge of the worth of their objection in the light of this answer. Turning from them, Christ called the crowd about Him again. This crowd had had no part in the attack by the Pharisees; they had come to learn, while their leaders had come to trap Christ. He gave the crowd the answer the Pharisees did not deserve, a principle rich in its implications, a rule of thumb by whose measurement they could instantly detect the pretensions of the rabbinical commands. "Hear ye me all, and understand. There is nothing from without a man that entering into him, can defile

Here, as explained in the Publishers' Note, Father Walter's manuscript ends, in the middle of a text. It is a text he was quoting from memory—Matthew 15:11: Not what goes into the mouth defiles a man, but what comes out; not the things he eats, but the word he utters.

Our Lord was very close to the end of His long Galilean ministry. Two great things remained, before He set out for Judaea, where He was to die. The first was the arrangement He made for the succession when He Himself should have left the earth—He announced that Peter was the rock upon which the Church was to be built and that to Peter the keys of the kingdom of heaven were to be given; He followed this immediately with the first explicit statement of the death He must die and of His Resurrection. The second was the Transfiguration, when He took Peter, James and John to Mt. Tabor and was there glorified before their eyes. On the way back to Capharnaum, He told the apostles once more of the suffering that was to come, adding the new detail that He was to be betrayed. There is a great mass of teaching at this time, directed mainly, it would seem, to the formation of the apostles themselves for the enormous task He had set them.

From then, Jesus was mainly in Judaea, where His enemies were wholly in control and His death was certain. His challenge to the rulers of the Jewish people, now open and continuous, was threefold. First, He taught (notably in the parables of the Prodigal Son, Dives and Lazarus, the Pharisee and the Publican, the Laborers in the Vineyard) that the Jews had forfeited their priority among the peoples of the earth, and He assailed the leaders themselves with increasing fierceness. Second, He asserted His own divinity. Third, He worked miracles, which the Pharisees knew they must disprove if He was not to carry all before Him. They made an immense effort of this sort in the case of the man born blind whom Jesus had healed. Then came the bringing back to life of the four-days-dead Lazarus of Bethany, brother of Martha and Mary. This was decisive for the Jewish leaders—both for the magnitude of the miracle, and the closeness to Jerusalem, Bethany being only a mile or two away: "If we let Him alone, all will believe in Him and the Romans will come and take away our place and nation." Orders were given that anyone who knew where He was should inform the leaders.

We come to the last week. The Pharisees were determined to take Him but dared not in the daytime, for fear of the people among whom He was moving and teaching freely. Their plan was to take Him by night, but each night He left the city. On the Saturday, Sunday and Monday nights He went to Bethany, to the house of Lazarus, Martha and Mary; on the Tuesday and Wednesday nights to Mt. Olivet. On the Saturday night at Bethany, He rebuked Judas. As He was coming into Jerusalem next morning, the crowd came out of the city to meet Him, strewed palms before Him and hailed Him as Son of David. On the Tuesday, His teaching was at its strongest and most terrifying. In the parable of the Wicked Husbandman He told how the Chosen People would kill God's own Son and how their inheritance would be given to the Gentiles. He uttered His longest denunciation of the Scribes and Pharisees. Upon Mt. Olivet that night, He told His followers of the destruction of Jerusalem and the end of the world.

On Wednesday, Judas made his bargain with the authorities to betray Jesus.

On Thursday, Jesus ate the paschal supper prescribed

by Jewish law, told the apostles of the sacrifice that by His death He was to offer His Father for the salvation of men, and made them priests of the new sacrifice in His own Body and Blood. From the supper-room, He went, as on the two previous nights, to Mt. Olivet, to a garden called Gethsemani. There He had His Agony, and conquered it. And there came Judas with a band of soldiers, to betray Christ with a kiss. He was dragged from court to court that night—twice He appeared before the Jewish leaders, and twice before the Roman governor, Pontius Pilate (with an appearance before Herod sandwiched in). In their own court, the Jews accused Him of claiming to be the Son of God: before Pilate they accused Him of disloyalty to Caesar. He was mocked and spat upon, thorns were twisted into a wreath and pressed into his head, he was scourged. They made Him carry His own cross to Calvary, a hill outside the city, nailed Him to it, and hung Him on it, between two thieves, one of whom repented and was promised Paradise. His mother and Mary Magdalen and John were there to the end. In three hours He died. His body was laid in a tomb nearby. On Sunday, the third day after that, He rose again from the dead.

The two chapters which remain in this book give Father Walter's own account of the Death and the Resurrection.

11

CHRIST THE VICTIM

IN HIS death on the cross, Christ gave the full human meaning of suffering and added to it the rich flavor of the divine. He was not merely submitting to suffering, making a virtue of necessity; He embraced suffering. So the graphic symbol of His last moments became the universal symbol of all His doctrine and His life. Those who watered down His doctrine in later centuries quite logically stripped the body from the crucifix; those who revolted against Him, trampled on the crucifix or made it a mockery. They were quite right. For on Calvary, by His cross, Christ gave the full statement of His way of human living, the full details for life to those who would come after Him. If we are to abandon His way of life, we should destroy the cross.

He Himself has said that the only way to follow Him was to take up the cross; and this has been astounding advice to human ears. It is strange to men that divine wisdom, in mapping out the best way for men to live, could hit upon no better way than that of the cross. This was not mere theory, even divine theory, for God took that royal road Himself; it was not a drastic exercise to round the spiritually flabby into shape, for He gave it to the most perfect of His friends—to Peter, James,

John, Magdalen, and His mother. His methods have not varied. The very special gift to the followers of Christ has always been a full cup of suffering; their response to His gift has always been as astounding as the death of the Author of life on the barren hill of Calvary. To them, suffering was not a thing to be cringed from in terror; it was not a brutal dose to be taken in dull stupidity; rather, it was a share in and a completion of the works of the Master, to be joyfully embraced, a vital help to others, a safe, sure, short way to heaven. Above all, it was an opportunity for the concrete expression of love, for sacrifice.

On Calvary, Christ's way of dealing with suffering and death was mocked as evidence of effeminate weakness by those whose god was brute strength. The hedonists of the time, whose norm was pleasure, recoiled from it. The intellectually proud, who could not see beyond the walls of the world, looked on with pity or indifference.

The men of the world have not changed much since then. The Cross of Christ is still seen as an exhibition of weakness, a shocking, revolting thing, or a needless, useless loss. This paradox of a suffering and dying God is not to be understood by the world. The initial paradox was bad enough, that He who had come that men's joy might be full should leave a prescription of suffering. The consequences of it have been positively bewildering: for the most joyous people in the world are those who most eagerly embrace suffering for themselves; yet these willing victims are the most thoughtful, the most kind, the most pitying towards suffering in others. But, then, isn't this a fairly exact correspondence with the Model who had time and heart, even in His agony, to continue the work of healing the sick, comforting the distressed, forgiving sinners, and providing for the lonely hearts of the world?

The secret of this paradox, as of all the paradoxes of Christian action, is to be found in the union of the divine and the human. Those of Christ's own life flowed from the substantial union of human and divine nature in the Person of the Word of God; those of the twentieth century's Christian life take their rise in the participation of divine life by men through grace. Of course Christianity is a puzzling phenomenon to those who know nothing of God and little of man. The full implications for human living of the crucified Christ are gathered only by one who knows both God and man and spends a lifetime of contemplation, with divine assistance, of both.

It is certainly true that any appreciation of the paradox of Calvary depends upon a humble study of the union of the human and divine in that tragedy. A whimper of pain immediately awakes some pity in us, for pain is well within the field of our own experience; when we have traced it down and found that a man and not a dog is suffering, our appreciation of the pain is deeper, our pity more profound, for we know how much more it means to a man to suffer than to a mere animal. On Calvary, we are trying to understand something of the sufferings of God. The work of this chapter is to look at the passion of Christ in itself, to see what it means for a God-man to suffer.

Obviously Christ did not have to suffer as the sea has to roar in a wild wind; He did not have to suffer as a man is forced to stand upright because he is lashed to a post. Had Christ not passed through the hands of His enemies untouched when they tried to seize Him earlier in His life? Even there in the Garden of Gethsemani, the crowd that had come roaring out for His blood fell down at the mention of His name. On His own word, he could have had twelve legions of angels when God knows one alone would have been more than enough. His word had called the world into being; and men came to reduce Him to helplessness with swords and clubs! What stupid weapons for a battle with God!

It is essential that we see clearly that Christ was not forced into His passion. What necessity was involved was that of a means to an end, the necessity a man is under to walk across the street if he is to get to the other side. Man was to be freed from sin, the humanity of Christ was to be exalted, the prophecies of Scripture to be fulfilled; and the passion and death of the Saviour were the means by which these things were to be done. This is not a denial of the possibility of other means to attain these ends; the point is that this is the way that had been decided on by God, and God's are not changing plans accommodating themselves to last-minute information pouring in from the ends of the earth.

His choice, then, of the means to the end of the Incarnation was a supremely wise, eternal choice. The passion and death of the Son of God were the best ways to obtain the things for which the Incarnation took place. The point is worth stressing. Perhaps we can understand it by a glance at the reasons for the superiority of the modern transparent, compact, extremely light raincoats for women over a raincoat made, let us say, of sheet-iron. The latter would certainly keep out the rain and so attain the chief end of a raincoat; but it would be folded into a hand-bag with extreme difficulty, would hardly be beneficial to the clothes beneath it, and might easily wear off a few layers of skin. It would certainly be no help to the disposition in hot weather, and would be an irritating thing to find draped over a chair. The modern raincoat contributes many more things by which the end of all raincoats can be more fittingly attained. The Christ-child might have glanced around His stable nursery, given one baby smile, of infinite worth because He was God, and then returned to eternal glory. This would have been more than sufficient to redeem men, to attain the principal end of the Incarnation. But would that divine smile have produced all the other things which pertain to the salvation of men over and above the forgiveness of sin?

Would it, for example, have given them that unanswerable protestation of limitless divine love that would stop their human hearts and start them off again in a rapid, eager beat as they attempted to respond to that love? Would men have had that terrifying estimate of the price of their souls, with its consequent conviction of the grave necessity for avoiding sin? Would it have flashed before men's eyes the living examples of humility, obedience, constancy, and justice that were struck out from the flint of the cross? Would it have sent men down the ages with their shoulders a little straighter, their heads a little higher, their step a little firmer in the knowledge that man, who had been conquered by the devil, had turned about and given his enemy a beating; that man, who had merited death, had conquered death by dying on a cross?

That cross against the sky with its arms flung out to the world was not a *beau geste*. It was not the exaggerated declaration of love from a cavalier professional in these matters. Hung between the earth and the sky, the blood that edged slowly down its rough surface to the earth beneath it consecrated the ground men walked on, while its arms purified the air as if to say a new world had been made. It stood there on the brow of the hill in a bold, challenging rebuke to the fears of men. This was the worst men could do and it could not stop the triumph of a Man; what, then, is to be feared from men? By the fruit of a tree, men had met defeat; by the bitter fruit of this tree, they conquered. Here was the new Moses with arms outstretched, praying. Here was a new rod, striking not the living rock but the very gates of heaven to swing them wide and loose a flood of grace upon the hearts of men.

Fighting men returning from war usually bring back a full quota of strange and interesting stories. It is to be noticed, however, that the stories revolve around the comic side of army life, the strange customs of foreign peoples, the compelling beauty of strange lands. These men have practically nothing to say of suffering and death. It is hard to go into the details of these things. It is much harder when the subject of the suffering is not merely a companion in arms but a companion in heart. St. Thomas Aquinas, for all his reputation as a cold-blooded metaphysician, showed this same reticence when he came on slow feet to the very cross itself and looked at the divine Victim. He makes no attempt to detail every suffering of Christ; indeed, what human word could contain them, what human heart hold them? Rather, Thomas adheres to a generalization of Christ's sufferings, to a classification rather than a description of them.

Looking at the cross through the eyes of Thomas, it is evident to us, as it was to him, that there is no question of Christ facing the evils which affect the soul directly, such evils as sin or the loss of grace. Nor could there be question of such intrinsic evils as sickness or the corruption of the body. What Christ suffered was brought upon Him from extrinsic sources. In this sense, Christ underwent all suffering.

Not that Christ underwent every individual suffering. Even the ingenuity of hate has its limitations. The officers of Elizabeth had to work fast to complete the sentence of hanging, drawing and quartering. Had a few more details, such as drowning, poisoning, shooting, scalding and overeating been added, their complete obedience would have been impossible. Add a few modern touches, such as airplane crashes, train wrecks, plunging from skyscrapers, and it is fairly easy to see that no one man can possibly undergo every individual suffering. What Christ suffered was every *kind* of suffering. His passion was the work of Jews and gentiles, of men and women, of princes and their officials, of priests and people, of friends and enemies. What can a man suffer? Well, he can be deserted by his friends. He can be stripped of his reputation, robbed of respect and honor. He can lose his possessions, even his very clothes. His soul can be weighed down by the weariness of distaste, by fear, by sorrow. His body can be beaten and wounded. It was in this sense of a man utterly stripped that Christ hung naked on the cross.

A man's body can be made to suffer in a great variety of ways. His head, for instance, might be crowned with thorns, his hands and feet transfixed by nails, his face beaten and spit upon, his whole body torn by lashes. He might suffer in his sense of touch, in his sense of smell, as by dying in a place long used as a depository of dead criminals, the place of skulls; his ears might be assailed by insults, obscenities, blasphemies; and his eyes might reveal to him the course of the tears streaming down his mother's face as she watched him suffering all these things. All these could happen to a man; all of them did happen to Christ.

He suffered every manner of suffering and His sufferings were greater in intensity than any other the world has seen. Understand, we are still viewing the Victim under that merciful light of generality. It is quite possible that some other man be crowned with sharper thorns or carry a cross a greater distance; the question here is not of this or that suffering but of all these sufferings taken together in a subject Who was the Son of God. We have some notion of the intensity of Christ's sufferings even if we stop at their universality and the slow, exceedingly painful relief that comes through death by crucifixion.

A more penetrating light is thrown on this intensity of suffering if we keep in mind the interior sufferings of Christ. It must be realized that He was bearing the sins of all the world, bearing them with a wisdom and charity that brought the full horror of sin, every sin, directly before His eyes. We must appreciate something of the torment of His soul when we remember that He could look into the very souls of His executioners and disciples as they sinned; and He was God to whom nothing is more hateful than sin. This last point, the subject of these sufferings, brings out fully the length to which God will go in search of love from men. Knowing that this man was God, we can know with what suffering the Man Christ saw the slow approach of death, the loss of this life which was above all other lives, the life of God. The wine at Cana had astonished the master of the feast for, like all things miraculously produced, it was perfect. So was this miraculously produced body of Christ endowed with the keenest of senses, the sharpest responsiveness of appetite; it was most perfectly fitted to respond thrillingly to the lightest touch of joy and, by that very fact, to shudder with the utmost of agony under the brutal blows of pain.

In other men, pain may be assuaged by reason; the martyrs, for example, in their ecstasy could be insensible to pain, or a woman in labor be joyful in her pain thinking of the child who will soon be in her arms. A child might even rejoice a little in the misfortune of having to have a sliver removed from its finger, considering the reward promised for submitting bravely to the process. There was none of this in Christ. He would not permit it; rather, He insisted that every faculty operate to its fullest for the redemption of man. All this suffering was in the most complete sense *voluntary*. He took upon Himself the amount and degree of suffering proportionate to the fruit that suffering was expected to bear—nothing less than the redemption of all men from all sin; proportionate, that is, to the sins of all the world. That He should have died so soon, after only three hours of agony, could be a surprise only to those who did not know what suffering He was undergoing, only to those who did not understand that this was the perfect Son of Mary who was redeeming the world.

In insisting on the universality and supreme intensity of the suffering of Christ, Thomas is not forgetting that Christ enjoyed the beatific vision, the joy of heaven. This in no way interfered with or lessened the tragedy of Calvary; rather, the very absence of its resonance in the body of Christ is just one more word in the long recorded testimony of divine love.

The superior reason of man is not a direct subject of sorrow; its object is truth. It becomes involved only in the suffering of the whole man. And it is by this superior reason that man sees God in heaven. Christ on the cross did not suffer directly in this superior reason; but intolerable suffering came to it indirectly from the suffering of the whole man. At the same time, the limitless joy of the vision was in Christ's will, but dammed up lest one trickle of it relieve the suffering offered for men. In heaven, the flood of that vision to the body is such as to spiritualize the material, to glorify the body with the radiance that was seen in the transfiguration of Christ; but on Calvary, this played not the smallest part in relieving the suffering of the body of Christ.

Death seems so far removed from the young that it is particularly hard to watch a young man die. Christ died a young man, in His early thirties. There was this comfort in His dying: since he surrendered that life in the name of love, there could never again be any question of the unconditional character of that love. The perfect age of thirty is a sad time to die. But it is the right time to bring out the full, deliberate offering of a life for love.

The hill upon which Christ died is just outside the old walls of the city of Jerusalem. It rises sharply from the very foot of those walls to a height that is just about level with the top of the old walls, and so close that a man could easily throw a stone from the wall to the brow of the hill or, peering a little, could read the inscriptions over the crosses of the criminals dying on the hill. Jerusalem was the place for Christ to die, for Jerusalem was a royal city and He was a king; Jerusalem was the killer of the prophets and He was the greatest of the prophets. According to St. Thomas, Jerusalem was the center of the world, the navel of the universe; and this is certainly true if we are speaking of the world of the spirit. It was a fitting place for Him to die whose death was to have repercussions to all the ends of the earth. He died outside the walls as the scapegoat of humanity, rejected and outcast by His people.

He hung on the cross between two thieves. Perhaps that special touch of disgrace was added in the hope that the people whom He had loved and healed, comforted and forgiven would identify Him with these criminals; if so the hope was vain. Ever since, the world has talked of His cross with hardly a word for the other crosses; kings have searched for and found and carried His cross, particles of it are still adored throughout the world. The others? They have played their part. They clustered around that central cross as around a judgment seat and heard a divine sentence passed. They showed to all men that suffering can be a soaring flight direct to heaven, or a weight pressing us down deeper into hell; for it was from the vantage point of a cross that one criminal recognized the throne and royal robes of the King, while the other saw only a dying criminal who could be safely mocked.

Christ, dying on the cross, was a willing victim but He did not kill Himself. It was not Christ Who stripped off His garments, drove the nails into His hands, or the spear into His side. His enemies could and did kill Him; but only because He submitted to them. He could have rendered them impotent or, submitting, He could have brought His body unscathed through their feeble, human gestures of attack. He did neither. Life was not so much being taken from Him as being laid down by Him. Not envy, not hatred, not the power of His enemies, but the obedience and love of the victim tells the real story of His sacrifice; He was obedient even unto death. An unwilling sacrifice is no sacrifice at all; surely, it is not the means of such a sweeping reconciliation as Christ planned. Man had lost God by disobedience; here, God was regained by the obedience of a Man.

Christ laid down His life in obedience to the command of His Father; the obedience, like the command, was inspired by an infinite love for men. That obedience brought out the terrible severity of divine justice's refusal to forgive sin until the penalty had been undergone; at the same time, it revealed the infinite goodness of God Who sent His only-begotten Son into the world to die that men might escape the penalty of their sin. With the help of His own people, Christ was handed over to the Gentiles to be put to death; salvation follows the same course, from the Jews to the Gentiles, not for the destruction of God but for the happiness of man.

Strictly speaking, there were very many who had a part in Christ's death, but their roles were vastly different. His Father gave Him over to death moved by justice, goodness, and love for men. The Son surrendered to death from that same goodness, and from obedience. Judas betrayed his Master from greed; the Jews betrayed Him from envy. Pilate handed Him over to the mob because of a cowardly fear that made him tremble at the name of Caesar. The surrender of the Father and the Son will be praised for all eternity; the acts of the others will be condemned without end.

True, there was some little excuse for the Romans. What did they know about the Messias and His coming? What interest did they have in the rumors they had heard of the wonders worked by Christ? There was even some excuse for most of the mob that hooted at the heels of Christ up to Calvary; and then slunk away in terror to their homes. They had none of the expert knowledge of the Scriptures that would enable them to judge of Christ independently; even though they had been impressed and enthusiastic about His life and works, it was the function of their leaders to approve and disapprove. They themselves were easy subjects of deception.

But the leaders of the people—there is a different story. They had the Scriptures and they knew them. They had followed the works of Christ in detail and had examined them with expert eyes. They had the norms of discrimination between the works of God and the works of men. Like all the others gathered on Calvary to kill Christ, they did not know He was the Son of God; but they, above all others, should have known. They could have known only by faith; but they did not receive the faith that would allow their eyes to pierce the veil of His humanity because they did not want that faith. They put the impediments of hate, envy, and deceit in the way of faith; and only those of good will can see the things that belong to the eyes of God.

On them, as they wished, rests the blood of this innocent Man. Theirs was the greatest sin, a sin in itself greater than any other that can be committed. As we pass down the line of the executioners, the sin becomes less, for the norm of gravity in sin will always be the malice of the will; that malice lessened definitely after Judas and the princes of the people, coming down in a steadily decreasing degree to the common people, Pilate, and the Roman soldiers.

Some one has defined the efficiency of modern transport as the ability to get us a long way quickly so that we can start back sooner. This is really more than jest; it is an epitome of the fact and the vanity of our worship of activity. We have actually come to the irrational stage of seeing positive virtue in rush, hurry, aggression. As a corollary of that, there is pity in our hearts for the poor people who are condemned to live their lives in one place, particularly a small place. To our minds, what a man does with his hands, his feet, or even his brain, are all-important; we do not at all appreciate what a man can do with his heart. To the thorough modern, then, Christ on the cross is a picture of utter helplessness, of complete frustration; He could not go anywhere, could not get anything done. A religious-minded modern might ponder sadly on what those helpless hands of Christ might have done, what words the swollen tongue might have spoken, what sinners might have been sought out by the transfixed feet. As a matter of fact, it was when Christ was so helplessly fixed to the cross that He got the most done.

Divinity has certainly gone to extreme lengths to bring us to our senses, to a realization that in rushing around the world we are only circling back to the place from which we started. We move in circles, inevitably, unless it is our heart that moves. All that Christ had done in those busy three years in which He had not so much as time to eat, was as nothing compared to what He accomplished on Calvary. Just when the full causality of the God-man was unleashed, men stood mocking or pitying His helplessness. From that cross, Christ's divinity operated as the efficient cause of all the wide effects produced by the passion of Christ in the lives of men; Christ's human will, from the deep roots of grace and charity, merited all those effects; His flesh satisfied for the punishment due to our sins, freed us from the slavery of sin, and was the means of sacrifice by which we are reconciled to God. The efficient, the meritorious, the redemptive, the satisfactory, and sacrificial causality of the redemption of men flowed out from a man dying on a cross. This was God's way of getting things done.

A modern true to his training would immediately object that as far as could be observed, all that Christ did on Calvary was to die in disgrace and tear out the hearts of His friends. Just what did Christ get done there? To understand the difficulty of answering that question to the satisfaction of the twentieth century, as well as to appreciate how far we have drifted today from the goals of men, it is only necessary to reflect for a moment on how little the revolutionary effects of Christ's passion mean to the modern world. What do these things mean today: liberation from sin, freedom from the power of the devil, release from the punishment due to sin, reconciliation with God, the opening of the gates of heaven, and the exaltation of the God-man, Christ? What a snicker such a litany would win in Union Square! What reasons for a man to die!

Yet, it is only by these effects that a man can win the fight of his life. Indeed, it is only the thoughtfulness of divinity and the divine respect for the powers of man that still keep every man's fight his very own. These effects of Christ have been won for us; but we must allow their application in our own lives. The life of man is a battle he must win himself, one that is worth winning for himself as an individual, but one that he can win only because God died on a cross. And the world shrugs in indifference!

When Christ bowed His head and died, His life ended, as every man's does, by His soul leaving His body. But it is a serious mistake to see that dead body in the arms of His mother as so much human wreckage, a mass of matter destined for corruption. The soul of

Christ was not a tow-rope hooking His body to divinity any more than His flesh was a chain tying His soul to divinity. There was no intermediary of that union of God and human nature; the union was immediate and by reason of the Person. As He was taken down from the cross and during those three days of death, the Person of the Son of God and His divinity were still intimately united to that body, still intimately united to that soul, even though soul and body were separated. This Person did not result from the union of body and soul, nor from the union of human and divine nature; this was an eternal Person, not to be destroyed by the destruction of the union of body and soul. What God took, He kept. That grace of union, like all grace, could be lost only by sin; and there was no more sin in the dead Christ than in the living one.

In this light, the care and love given to the dead body of Christ, the courage of Joseph of Arimathea in demanding it of Pilate, the sorrow of His mother receiving it from the cross, were more than the reverence that springs from loving memories. Everything suffered by that dead body, even though it were only the caress of love, had infinite value for the souls of men. It is true, of course, that during those three days, Christ was dead; that is, He was no longer man, for man is not a body, neither is he a soul, but a composite of the two. Here that composite had been dissolved. The dead body of Christ was a body without a soul; but otherwise it was exactly the same, still possessed by the same Person, still united to divinity through that Person. Christ had not merited death, but He took it; He had not merited corruption of the body, and this He would not take lest there be any slightest doubt of His divinity.

Indeed, it was not at all fitting that that body should

suffer corruption; the fact that it did not has ever since been a serene comfort to men and an unanswerable refutation of Christ's enemies. It was a foregone conclusion that men would doubt Christ's death; even though Pilate sent a spear through His heart, and His tomb was sealed and guarded day and night. Precautions such as these cannot stop the doubts of men when doubt seems so much more comfortable a thing than belief; even though it may be necessary to stoop to stupidity by hiring sleeping witnesses to testify to events happening during their sleep, such men will have their doubts. Either Christ's death or His resurrection must be rejected under penalty of accepting every single detail of His life and doctrine. For us, who have no doubts, there is comfort in watching Christ placed in the tomb; from that time on, men could watch those they loved placed in a tomb and remember that the doors of every tomb are not eternally locked, that every tomb has an exit as well as an entrance, that it is a gate rather than the end of a road.

Perhaps, too, the burial of Christ was to remind us that we are to die to sin by Baptism, to be buried from the world, and separated from the inordinate passions of men. Christ was in that tomb for two nights and a day that we might know it is a double death, the death of sin and the death of the body, that we escape by Baptism and its full consummation.

As His body drooped on the cross with the breath of life gone out of it, the soul of Christ descended into hell; not to the hell of the damned, but to the hell which we call Limbo. There was already confusion and despair enough in the devil's kingdom as the knowledge of His victory became more apparent; in Limbo the souls of the just awaited the opening of the gates of life by the death of the Author of life. It is not at all strange to us that Our Lord's first thought in death would be for others, as all the thoughts of His life had been. Only God knows how long the centuries had seemed, waiting there in Limbo; perhaps that was why He hurried so. Surely, only God can tell us of the hilariously joyful reception given the Saviour of the world by those who tasted the first fruits of His sacrifice.

When the short visit was over, there would be a little note of sadness such as perpetually dogs the steps of sin. For there would be souls in Purgatory who had not yet satisfied for their sin and these could have no part in His triumphant possession of His kingdom until the last farthing had been paid; the souls in Limbo would still bear the stain of original sin, and so could never enter that kingdom. As for the damned in hell, He had not come to them, He had nothing to bring them, not the slightest bit of their punishment was relieved. They had chosen, and held fast to their choice; not even the Conqueror, the Master of the universe, the God of all, forces the human will to change even so stupidly disastrous a choicc as this.

Mary, on the arm of John, went down from the hill and its sepulchre into a city empty of Christ; but she carried with her the secret that would change forever the view of men on suffering and death. To Mary and John, the mystery of death and suffering was cleared up by faith: its finality was done away with by the knowledge that it was the beginning of a new life; its corruption was more than matched by the glorification of the body that was the ultimate goal of death; death's inevitability was more than made up for by the certitude of immortality.

In other words, they entered that empty city in full

possession of the Christian philosophy of suffering and death. They had learned from the dead Christ that suffering was to be joyfully embraced yet to be mercifully and constantly relieved in others. They knew now that suffering would be their lot in order that their joy might be full; that the way of the cross, for all its sorrows, was a joyful road leading to fuller, and perpetual, joy.

In sharp contrast to this, the materialistic philosophies of their age still shuddered before the sight of suffering and the terror of death. To them, suffering and death still remained mysterious, something for the most part hated, yet, paradoxically, something that is quite willingly inflicted upon others. Those philosophies were then, as they have been ever since, apparently dedicated to pleasure and to flight from pain; yet in actual fact, they were philosophies of gloom and pessimism not only to the victims sacrificed to their ends, but to the very champions of these philosophies.

Mary and John, and all who would come after them, faced suffering and death, not only as men and women, but as men and women who had been made partakers in the life of God. Their materialistic contemporaries, and ours, faced these mysteries of pain and death, not as participators in the life of God, not even as men and women, but in a fashion worthy only of something less than a man. Really, it should have been so; the basic differences of the two views clearly would allow nothing less sharply contrasted. To the Christian, the victim, the sufferer who dies, is in reality a sovereign master, wielding even such terrible weapons as his own pain and death for his own high purposes, rising above the material and what the material can inflict upon him, always carrying within himself that spark that gives him independence of all that is less than the spirit. In the other view, the sufferer is simply and solely a victim of superior forces; he is beaten, vanquished. There is nothing within him to give him title to independence of the forces that crash upon him to his destruction; he is the slave of obviously superior forces; his outlook is one of hopeless despair.

In fact, the materialist has no reason for fighting against hopeless odds. He has no place to go, no goal worthy of suffering, nothing worth the price of death. The one thing he knows is the life he has in his hands, and he knows precious little about that; to preserve it, he should logically go to any lengths, scruple at no means, however base. On the other hand, the follower of Christ along the way of the cross aims at goals that are not only worthy of a man; they are goals proper to God, goals so far superior to anything material as to make the loss of any material things, or all of them, a mere trifling price to pay. The Master's question still remains unanswerable: "What shall it profit a man if he gain the whole world and suffer the loss of his own soul?" His incredible promise still holds: "He that shall lose his life shall find it." For there are some things worth the price of all the suffering a man can endure, even of all the sufferings that the God-man could endure; and there are some things to which death is not a threat but a gateway.

The world of our time, or of any time, gazing on the Son of God dead on the cross, looks at a willing Victim who conquered, at a Man who died and, dying, conquered death, at a Man who wrote in the indelible words of infinitely precious acts a fundamentally important lesson for all men to read. There it is written, never to be erased, that the spiritual is superior to the material, that all things in man's life, even life itself, are to be ordered to the good of his soul. In the crucifix, the universal symbol of the life, doctrine, and death of Christ, He has left us the whole book of divine wisdom for human living. It is a compact thing, readily scrutinized by the most ignorant, though it is never exhausted by the most wise and the most holy. It has been the book of the saints. In that book there is the answer to the enigma of suffering and to the horror of death. There is the ultimate chapter on human living by the divine Exemplar of human life.

✣ 12

THE CONQUEST OF DEATH

TO A young doctor just beginning his practice, or a young married couple setting out on their common life, it seems impossible that anyone can ever get too old to dream. In a sense they are right; but it is true that it is the youth of a man that is filled with dreams. As adolescence changes into manhood and womanhood, vast horizons open up to give birth to the dreams of the young. The long, wide roads are faced with a tingling joy of anticipation; yet in the very midst of the grand dreams of conquest, there is often a note of misgiving, a tinge of fear on venturing into this huge new world.

If this fear actually takes precedence, an unhealthy state of indecision develops, spelling the end of effort, of accomplishment, even of life in the human sense of hearty living. On the other hand, if that fear is kept healthy, it is an invaluable check-rein on our plunging hearts, keeping them from running wild by insisting on caution and some measure of prudence in even our boldest efforts.

This strange mingling of joy, anticipation, and fear seems to be the common note of all the goals that open up new roads, the ends which are beginnings. It seems to be the genius of our nature to be forever seeking wider, longer, harder goals, to approach them with mingled joy and fear; yet to be stagnated, stifled without them. All this is, of course, true of the goal of death which opens up the horizons of eternity. From this point of view, the story of Our Lord's resurrection was particularly well told, with its note of fear on the part of the soldiers, of great joy on the part of the disciples; for the combination of these two is typical of the emotions of every man as he reaches an end that starts him off again on a new road.

There is reason enough for joy in Christ's conquest of death, for it tore down the wall at the end of life's last blind alley, lifting the barrier of finality which lies heavy across the path of every human heart. A barrier is always a source of suffering for a human heart with its innate drive for newer, wider, higher goals, and which never has enough of traveling, since it was made for the infinite. When the last door, the door of death, swings wide, there is an immediate, joyous release from the haunting fear that perhaps there is an end of love, of knowledge, of accomplishment, and of all the other things that the human heart treasures; the fear that what a man presses on to so desperately for all of a lifetime may yet be taken away from him.

It is quite certain that life is not long enough by far. Youth surely does not know the deep values hidden in the roar and confusion of life; it takes time to appreciate these things, since we learn so very slowly. Life is a cathedral which must be visited many times to get more than a dim appreciation of the beauty of its lines; it is a masterpiece that must be looked at lovingly hour after hour, day after day, if our eyes are to see the soul of it; it is a book to be read again and again, each reading giving its lines new significance, new depths. When life is nearly over we begin to put proper values on such familiar, homely things as spring sunshine and the pure beauty of winter. Not even then have we more than scratched the surface of the mystery of love, of sacrifice, of selfless family life, and God's hovering benevolence. We need more time. It would not do to lose life just as we begin to penetrate its worth.

Yet, seeing this door of death swing wide into a new life, there is, too, a distinct and healthy note of fear in facing the endless stretches that will satisfy our hearts. For if death is conquered and life goes on forever, while the good is preserved, the record of evil, too, has to be faced. Man cannot wipe out his deeds with the help of a faulty memory; he must face his life, all of it, with responsibility for the evil as well as with pride and affection for the good. The man who is utterly fearless at such a prospect is somewhat of a fool. Briefly, the conquest of death not only opens up the possibilities of heaven but also of hell; it guarantees judgment, complete and accurate casting up of all accounts.

This is a fearful truth for a man; it is insupportable for a coward. To some men of every age, the news of Christ's resurrection has been bad news, so bad as to drive them to the childishly irrational extreme of refusing to read the news as though that would destroy it. A prospective lawyer who would burn the report of his bar examination for fear of learning that he had failed would soon discover that he could not begin his practice simply because he had destroyed that report; the men who refuse to read the news of Christ's resurrection must ultimately learn that they cannot go out and live just because they maintained their ignorance of life. In actual fact, what they have done is to give fear the upper hand, ending all real effort, real accomplishment, real living by going on record as denying anything in life worth living for, worth the awful burden of responsibility.

In a strange paradox, these cowards who are afraid of life put their denial of life on the basis of pride and thus join hands with others whose pride has gone so far as to submerge even healthy fear. Both conclude to the supremacy of man. One, by releasing him, through a denial of responsibility, from answering to any superior; the other, by a strong, indignant rejection of dependence as a slur on human greatness: what we cannot reach by our human powers simply cannot exist.

It is hard for the hand, the eye, or the mind of a man to reach to the uttermost limits of truth; so hard, in fact, as to be impossible. Though the truth that the soul of man is undying can be reached and has been reached by the human mind, these men will have none of it. As for the resurrection of the body to eternal life, that is incredible. After all, we have only God's word for it; and we are not taking anyone's word for anything. We, they say, depend on no one. We live our own lives. We stand on top of the world. Though we had nothing to do with our own beginnings, though we have less to say about our own ending, though our knowledge of the space between these two is pitifully vague and our knowledge of the space beyond either beginning or end is necessarily second hand, we are supreme. After all, we can know more than a tree, a dog, or a cosmic force; so we must know all that can be known.

Pride and fear are no new things in human life. It is true that we have no record, in the story of Christ's resurrection, of the kind of fear we know so well today, the fear that destroys life in preference to living it. But we have a record of a pride that would go so far as to bribe witnesses to deny the uncomfortable truth. However, neither pride nor fear destroys truth. Christ rose again from the dead; man has his life to face, both its good and its evil.

In a sense, Christ had to rise from the dead. He had made the resurrection the test of the divinity of His mission; it was the supreme sign granted to the stiffnecks of His own generation. Without the resurrection, His doctrine and His life would have seemed to men only another episode in the long history of pseudoprophets, continuing to our own day, who promise to return shortly after death and whose disciples have kicked their heels while they waited, feeling more and more foolish, more and more angry at having been duped, until, finally, they stalk off, through forever with the master who did not keep his appointment.

The Mother of Christ, in her triumphant song, had said of God that He exalted the humble and brought down the mighty. Her Son had insisted "The first shall be last and the last shall be first"; "He that exalteth himself shall be humbled, and he that humbleth himself shall be exalted." He Himself had been humbled to the utmost degree, even to the disgraceful death on the cross. The exaltation of His resurrection was God's only fitting answer to the humiliation of Calvary.

The heavy hearts and slow steps of the disciples trudging to Emmaus are a faint picture of the feeble faith that would have flickered in the disciples of Christ had He not risen; Paul was right when he maintained that if Christ had not risen our faith would have been vain. Notice the bitter regret in the words of the two disciples making their way out of Jerusalem to escape the scene of their great disappointment; they explained to the risen Christ, whom they did not know, that they *had* hoped their Master was the Messias who had come to save all Israel. This is only a faint rumbling hint of the thunderous, crashing disappointment that would have come to the hearts of men if Christ had not risen, a disappointment the more disastrous because of the great heights to which the hopes of men had been raised.

The coaxing phrase which they addressed to Christ, "it is now toward evening and the day is far spent," is much more than a statement of the time of day; it is a threat of the approach of an eternal night over the hearts of men if their Master be not risen. On the contrary, the high hearts and eager steps with which they rushed back to Jerusalem, not waiting for rest or food, shows us faintly to what faith and hope, confirmed by the risen Christ, will reach: no hour is too late, no day too fatiguing, no journey too long. For we have risen from the death of sin and the bright goal of eternity lies invitingly before us.

A half-finished job may be a testimony to a man's good intentions; in deference to these, we sometimes blind our eyes and still our tongue before this pitiful evidence of man's wavering will. That half-finished job is, in fact, an unanswerable declaration that its author was a victim of impulse. Perhaps it is because he did not realize the backaches that must go into a garden that he must now survey a healthy crop of weeds; perhaps it is because he did not see the hardships involved in what Stevenson has called "domesticating the recording angel" that a man of today finds himself in a divorce court. At any rate, while impulse is a great beginner, it is a very poor finisher. God is not the victim of impulse. He never turns out a half-finished job, laughing it off or hiding it in confusion. What He starts, He finishes; that is why He started it. All this is, of course, true of our redemption. It is the work of God and so it is not left half-finished. Christ did not come merely to free us from evils, for that is only half the job; He came, finishing the job, to move us to good. Salvation means much more than throwing off the chains of sin; it means rushing forward to scale the walls of the kingdom of heaven. To achieve the first of these, Christ bore our evils for us; for the rest, He gave us a start, a goal, and an exemplar of the high things to be accomplished by the keen, sharp steel He put into our hands.

Perfect as the work of redemption might be with the full wisdom and power of divinity to guarantee its completion, men could still attempt to escape it. As is the way of God, He allowed men to go their tortuous way when they insisted on blinding themselves. But, again in His divine way, He foresaw and forestalled the vagaries of the human mind in its attempt to dodge a difficult truth. There was a human and divine nature in Christ; so, of course, some men would question His divinity, while others would doubt His humanity. God left no grounds for either uncertainty; if men must escape the truth, they would be forced to spin their doubts from the frail thread of falsehood.

If Christ had come out of the tomb as soon as the guards arrived, not giving them time to settle themselves for a long vigil, they might have questioned the reality of His death, considering it a conjuror's trick with the executioners playing the part of accomplices. If He had let weeks, months, or even years roll by, men might easily have forgotten about His death, have surrendered hope, and actually have questioned the resurrection when it did happen. It was, of course, for Christ to choose the moment of His resurrection. That absurd gesture of the cords tied about the hands of God in

Gethsemani was no more absurd than the solemn sealing of His tomb and the establishment of a soldier guard before it; as if the Omnipotent were to be held by bonds that are efficacious against men.

As a matter of fact, Christ had tried to ease the reception of the news of the miracle of His resurrection by what might be called the practice sessions or rehearsals: the resurrections of Lazarus, the son of the widow of Naim, and the saints who walked the streets of the Holy City after His death. He could not hope that men would accept the fact of a man walking from the tomb quite as nonchalantly as they do the fact of a man walking from the door of his house in the morning; but, at least, the shock of contact with divine power in meeting death might be eased enough so that the minds of men would not be numbed by it. Of course, these were merely rehearsals; these men who had risen from the dead had to die again, and men saw them die. Christ was the first Who rose from the dead immortal; He was the real conqueror of death. The rest of us are to share in that conquest but it was first accomplished by Him.

It is obvious that a dead man can do little for himself, otherwise he would certainly not put up with the banked flowers that cloy the air with sweetness. Man's re-entry, like his first appearance on life's stage, is not written into the script by man himself. Christ the man was as helpless as any other human being. In fact, once He had bowed His head and died, that Man no longer existed; His soul was separated from His body and their reunion could not be arranged by either the body or the soul. It is to be remembered, however, that divinity was still united to that dead body, still joined to that separated soul; the Person of the Son of God still possessed both the body and the soul. By the divine power of that Person, the soul and body could be reunited, and they were. Christ raised Himself from the dead. It was by His own power that the soul and body were reunited and the Man walked forth from the tomb: not in answer to a command, as did Lazarus; not raised up by the hand of another, as was the widow's son; but of His own power, for Christ was God.

All through this tract on the conquest of death by Christ, Thomas walks on the solid ground of divine authority. This is not material about which a man can afford to guess. These things are important. We must know them, and beyond all doubt, because they are the things that wait at the end of life and give it its fullest meaning. At that, Thomas's caution was no more than an imitation of the caution of God; for every detail of this conquest of death was expressly brought out by God Himself and carefully set down in His inspired writings. In this tract, every article of Thomas proceeds from an explicit text of Sacred Scripture.

From the darkness of the narrow tomb, through the daylight of that first Easter morning, came the same Man Who had died on the cross, possessed of the same body and the same soul. The body, kept incorrupt in the tomb for three days by divine power, was now reunited to the soul; the identical body that had been laid in the tomb by others now came forth by itself. There was no point in an apparent or fantastic body being shown to men that morning; that would mean that Christ had not risen and, as we have seen, Christ had to rise from the dead. Lest there be any doubt of the reality of that body of His, Christ invited the terrified disciples to "Touch me and see, that a spirit has not flesh and bones as I have." With the condescension to their defects, such as we make to the blind in allowing them to run their fingers over our face that they might feel what they cannot see, Christ allowed His disciples, spiritually blind, to feel what they could not believe they saw.

The body they touched, while the Son of God stood patiently suffering their incredulousness, was the same one they had seen nailed to a cross; now it was whole, integral, with every drop of blood lost in the passion recovered. Though Christ had come through closed doors, He allowed the disciples to touch Him; but even sight and touch were not enough. They must have been strange with Him, tense, pretty well incapable of speech; after all, one doesn't have much chance to practise talking to a man who has just died. At any rate, something was needed to break the ice, some little human thing that would put everyone at his ease; with that subtle divine graciousness that is a compliment in its benefactions, Christ asked the disciples if they had anything to eat. At once they were at home with Him again. They had hold of His arm, they were sitting at table with Him, talking to Him again after the nightmare at Calvary.

Though Christ's body was the same, it was now in a quite different condition. It was no longer capable of suffering, for it was a glorified, a spiritualized body with all the sublime qualities of a body completely subject to the soul. Now there was no longer any need, as there had been in the beginning, to stem the flow of the double glory of Christ's divinity and His human soul. Christ came through closed doors, walked with the disciples to Emmaus and they knew Him not; He was at table with them and, when He willed, they immediately recognized Him and He disappeared from their eyes. He could eat food but was not dependent on it. He could move from place to place with the speed of thought. One quality of a glorified body He kept hidden, lest it overwhelm them as it had on Tabor, and that was the splendor that shines through the body from the beatific perfection of the soul.

At our own resurrection, considerable repair work will be necessary. There will be broken noses to be straightened, lined faces to be smoothed out, missing teeth to be recovered, gnarled hands to be returned to the fine beauty of youth. There was none of that repair work necessary in Christ. His body, being miraculously formed, had been perfect. The one thing that might have been done, the removal of the awful scars of the passion, was left undone; these scars were no longer awful but rather things of striking beauty. They were a badge of merit, an eternal prayer for men, a declaration and an inspiration to courage and unquestioning love. They were identifying marks that would be worn in their turn by thousands of men and women who literally took up His cross; to others, who would refuse that cross, they would be an eternal rebuke, as unanswerable as unrequited love.

When we speak of the witnesses of the resurrection, following the lead of Scripture which itself uses the word, we must be careful to understand what is meant by the phrase. The resurrection of Christ was not the sort of thing that could be seen or tested by human means. Our knowledge has a wide scope, but it also has a limit; certainly, one of its limits is marked by the tombstone. What we know of the future life, we know, not by human investigation, but by being told, that is, through revelation; and the resurrection of Christ, being well beyond the milestone of death, certainly pertains to the future life.

We can see the punishment and pains of life; so men witnessed the passion of Christ. We see public rewards, and reasonably so, for these stir other men on as punishments give them pause. But the punishments and rewards that follow on death are not administered in a market place for all to see. They are God's secrets; through His goodness, they are told to some that the good news may be spread. So it was with the resurrection; it was not a public fête but rather the mystery of an Easter dawn.

We know nothing whatsoever of Christ's first visit with His mother, though merely on human grounds, leaving aside His divine thoughtfulness, we can have no doubt that His first appearance was to her. We do know, however, that, of all His other appearances, the first was to a woman, Mary Magdalen. That appearance was the climax of a story which has meant more to sinners than anyone but God can tell, showing them what they know deep in their own hearts, namely, that their capacity for great love is not less but more than their capacity for great sin. Even on Calvary, Magdalen had hardly reached such heights of loyalty, of unselfish devotion, and complete, unquestioning love. Of all His followers, she alone received the risen Christ without question; in that scene there was no room for explanations, for protestations, for demands. He merely said, "Mary"; instantly, joyously, she responded in words that left nothing to be said: "My Master."

One turns from the scene regretfully, as though much more had been missed than had been seen, so much was there to see. Outstanding is the delicate thoughtfulness of God balancing womanhood's accounts; a woman had begun the sad story which ended in man's death, now a woman began the glad story of this Man's conquest of death. Then, too, there is the divine recognition and appreciation of human love. This woman had been faithful even to the end: when the disciples scattered before the threat of Calvary, she was under the cross; when they huddled in fear and doubt in Jerusalem, she was at the tomb; even though it was apparently empty, she clung to it, for it was all she had left of the Master to Whom she had given her heart. His first appearance to a woman was a rebuke and a refutation to the pride of men. For it is not by strength, power, or keenness of intellect that our place in the kingdom of God is determined; but by our success in living, a success which is measured by the heart's approach to God.

There were no eye-witnesses to the resurrection of Our Lord. True, the guards had good reason to suspect that something was happening: "there was a great earthquake; for an angel of the Lord came down from heaven, and drawing near rolled back the stone, and sat upon it. His countenance was like lightning, and his raiment like snow. And for fear of him the guards were terrified, and became like dead men." One can understand their terror; but it was terror of an angel, not of the risen Christ. The picture of a glorious Christ stunning the heavily armed soldiers by His splendor is more an artistic summary of the whole significance of the resurrection than a portrayal of the fact. This resurrection exceeded all human knowledge; it could be learned only from above. As the order of divine providence has always been to lead the lower by the higher, men learned of the resurrection through the angel who sat on the stone where Christ was laid and answered men's unspoken questions: "Ye seek Jesus of Nazareth. He is not here. He is risen."

For themselves, and for the rest of the world, it was important that the disciples know, and know well, the facts of Christ's resurrection. In making it His personal business that they should know, Our Lord stressed two points: the truth of the resurrection and the glory of His risen body. The first He brought home to them by appearing to them, talking with them, eating and drinking with them, permitting them to touch His body. The second, that is, the fact that He had risen to a different life, He brought out clearly enough by showing His body's dominion over matter; and even more impressively, from the standpoint of the human heart, by His refusal to return to that life of constant social intercourse and familiarity which had marked all His days with them.

Superficially, it would seem a mark of much greater love for Him to give them the full measure of the comfort of His presence during the few days still left before His Ascension. Actually, however, that would have been a rather feeble, nearsighted love which could not look beyond the moment into the future, beyond the surface into the depths of the souls of the disciples. They might easily have fallen into the error, had He lived intimately with them again, that would hide the full sweep of life after death; they might have been satisfied that He was among them again, falling back into old ways, taking for granted that His life now was as it had been before. There was no chance for this when the Master was here only for a moment and gone again.

As it was, there was no time to get used to Christ, to begin to take Him for granted. He came from nowhere and disappeared as mysteriously. Locked doors, great distances offered Him no impediment. To some, He revealed Himself fully and clearly, matching the clear, solid faith in their minds with the clarity of His appearance; to others, it was only with a veil of mystery about Him that matched the veil of doubt and confusion that their tepid faith had allowed to drop before their eyes. Under such circumstances, they were always on tiptoe of mystery and expectation; their minds were sharp, their attention keen, their ears alert, faith digging deeper and deeper foundations in their hearts.

Christ did not attempt to argue His disciples into accepting the resurrection by overpowering them with syllogisms. This thing was not susceptible of proof; in its beginnings and in its goal, it was outside the whole scope of nature. What He did do again and again was to give them evident signs of His resurrection, signs of the credibility of the mystery. The signs were indeed necessary, for their hearts were not easily disposed to belief; their very slowness and stubbornness adds a force and validity to their testimony which place it above all suspicion by those who came after them through the centuries. In a real sense, we might say that all men put their hands into the side of Christ along with Thomas.

There was an abundance of these signs sufficient to satisfy the most exacting, the sort of abundance we have come to expect from God. There was, for instance, the testimony of the angels and that of Scripture to the fact of the resurrection. To assure men of the reality of His risen body, Christ did everything but put Himself under a microscope: the apostles saw His body, they touched it, they even put their hands into His side and their fingers into the wounds of His hands and feet. In testimony to the living character of this body, to its being vivified by a soul, Christ performed all the operations proper to man: on the side of the nutritive powers, Christ ate and drank; on the side of the sensitive powers, He saw and heard His disciples, answering their questions, saluting them; on the intellectual side, Christ discoursed with them, and explained the Scriptures. On the divine side, He showed the possession of divine power by the miracle of the fishes the apostles found already broiling on the shores of the Lake of Galilee when they scrambled from their boat to greet Him. To the glory of the resurrection, He brought the testimony of entrance through closed doors, invisibility or visibility as He willed, and so on. In view of all this, it would be an unreasonable man indeed who would doubt that it is reasonable to believe that the Son of God had risen from the dead.

It is a truth well worth the believing. For it is the model, the exemplar of every other resurrection. Indeed, it is the cause that lies behind the rise of the countless thousands of men who have lived and died, and will live again; this is the fact that changed the rock at the door of the tomb from a blocking boulder to a triumphal arch. Perhaps we can see this best if we look at the life, death, and resurrection of Christ as an integral whole, as indeed they were, destined to destroy death and restore life. This whole was the instrument used by the first cause, divinity itself: thus the life, passion and death of Christ were the common instrumental causes of both the conquest of death and the beginning of eternal, glorious life; His resurrection, by way of exemplar, was the cause of the destruction of our death and the restoration of our life to immortality.

In exactly the same way, the resurrection of Our Lord is the cause and exemplar of an even more wonderful resurrection that goes on about us every day: the resurrection of the soul from the death of sin to the life of grace. That spiritual tomb is sealed by our choice of sin; it is guarded, not by the soldiers of Rome, but by the legions of Satan and the disorderly hordes of inordinate appetites, guards who do not fall asleep. Because Christ has risen, the soul can come forth from this tomb in its original splendor. Again, there are no witnesses; only the weeping Magdalen, our own soul, overcome at finding the Master and Friend once more.

We are never more conscious that we were not made for earth than after such a fresh resurrection from the tomb of sin; then, above all other times, we realize keenly that we are pilgrims, that our soul is a little lonely, a little out of place in a world of matter, a little anxious for the world of the spirit. In much the same way, the body of Christ was a little out of place after the resurrection; it did not belong in a world of corruptible bodies, for it had begun an immortal and incorruptible life. It belonged in a heavenly and incorruptible place. So, when the time of consolation and instruction of the apostles had come to its close, the Master took them to the top of the hill overlooking Jerusalem, said His last farewell, gave the last assignments that would keep His followers occupied to the end of time, and ascended into heaven. Behind Him He left a lonely, frightened, helpless group which was yet the nucleus for the conversion of the world. That group was so stupefied by His loss that it took an angel to get them back into the city; there, they huddled in fear of their lives for ten days in an upper room.

Had not Christ said He would be with them always? Yes. He was and He will be by His divine presence. But He also said, "It is better for you that I go," and He was right, as God is always right. This was the work of strong love, not of that coddling, imperfect, weak love that saps all the strength out of the one loved. It was better, much better. It would be hard for them ever again to tear their hearts away from the goal of heaven, for He took a large part of their hearts with Him. It would never be hard for them again to hope, knowing He had gone before to prepare a place. Now, indeed, their faith would have its full scope, resting utterly without question on His word alone. He had given them a few days of consolation; now they must stand on their own feet, through His help; not attached to creatures, not dependent on men, not holding even to such a lovable thing as familiar, human life with the Man Christ.

Christ rose to the heights of heaven by the same power by which He had come forth from the tomb. He ascended to a place above every other created thing, a place worthy of His grace, His merits, His dignity. The Head of the Mystical Body blazed the trail in glory as He did in suffering, preparing our way. He is the high-priest entering the holy of holies that He might constantly intercede for us, taking His rightful seat at the court of heaven as Master and Lord of all things, not forgetting us but rather sending us His divine gifts in new abundance. Of course He took our hearts with Him, deepening our reverence and awe for His glorious humanity, with no lessening of our faith, our love, our hope of one day standing before Him and saying with Thomas, but without his doubts, "My Lord and my God."

We may smile at the astonishing versions a child can give of the Apostles' Creed; but, after all, "Jack Dempsey shall come" does not sound so very unlike "from whence He shall come." It would be only just if the angels smiled at an adult's no less childish mistake of trying to picture the right hand of the Father. The phrase, of course, is not to be taken literally; it contains no slight to left-handed people, indeed, a left-handed God would be no more absurd than a right-handed one.

The phrase is a vivid metaphor with at least three senses. The right hand figuratively means the glory of divinity, the happiness of heaven, or the judicial position of the Judge of the world. For Christ, then, to sit at the right hand of the Father means that with the Father He has the glory, the happiness, and the judicial power of divinity. By His divine nature, Christ sits at the right hand of the Father inasmuch as He is equal to the Father; according to His human nature, He occupies that position because He is in possession of the divine goods of heaven in a more excellent degree than any one else in that kingdom. But it is precisely as judge that the risen Christ captures our fascinated eyes.

To be a judge, clearly it is not enough for a man to look like one, talk like one, or walk like one; he must have power. Even possessed of power, he is no judge whose judgment proceeds from anger, greed, or any other vice; he is a mock judge rendering mock judgment because he is not judging from justice. If these two, power and love of justice, are the predispositions to judgment, the very soul of it is the wisdom by which it proceeds. So true is this, that in human affairs that wisdom is not left to individual capacities; to the best of our ability, we embody our common wisdom in the law by which a judge must judge. The predispositions to judgment are evident enough in Christ: He is the head of all men, the Son of God, with complete power and jurisdiction; He had died for love of justice, the justice of His offended Father. But it is particularly on the third count, the wisdom which is the soul of judgment, that His pre-eminent title to judgeship is clear; He is the incarnate Wisdom, the Word of God.

It is true that judgment, as a work external to God, is common to the whole Trinity; it is attributed, however, to the Second Person as to divine Wisdom. God is always the first source of just judgment; but, as in this life the power of judgment is committed to men relative to those who are subject to them, so in heaven the power of judgment is committed to Christ the Man. After all, He was a man himself, living His life intimately with His fellows. His judgment, severe as it may be, will not taste so bitter coming from one of our own. It is eminently fitting that the risen bodies of men be brought before the First of the risen and the Cause of the resurrection of all others; then men can stand facing their Judge, looking into His eyes as they have loved or feared to do during life.

Even if Christ did not have title to judgeship on the grounds of His divine nature, even if His supreme dignity as Head of the Mystical Body, His superabundance of sanctifying grace, and so of justice, be put aside, there is still the strong title of His merits. He had earned that judgeship. It was just according to the justice of God that He should judge Who had fought so hard for that justice, and conquered; Who had subjected Himself to the judgment of men and tasted all the bitterness of their unjust judgment.

The sweep of the judgment of Christ staggers the mind. If we attempt to conceive of a judgment that takes in every detail of one human life, we must confess our failure. Extend that to all men living at any one instant, or, indeed, to a judgment of all men dying at any one instant, and we are overwhelmed by the massive detail involved. If we push it further to include all men who ever have lived and died or ever will live and die, and then go on to the myriads of the angelic host, at the same time realizing that we never have evidence for a complete judgment of any one human action because we cannot reach the hearts of men, it begins to dawn on us that judgment is God's work. Perhaps we had best leave the working out of it to him.

The angels have already faced judgment by the Son of God when, in the beginning of the world, they fought their fight and lost or won; yet, they must face another judgment, as every man must, for the details of their lives, like ours, are not finished for years, for centuries, perhaps even to the end of time. An attempt to judge the damage done by fire is futile until the fire is extinguished. Neither can the life of a man be judged until its very last effect is accomplished; it is often only after the passing of time, even of long periods of time, that we can determine whether those effects are ultimately good or bad.

Our lives, you see, are not contained within the narrow boundaries of our years. Our smallest actions, because they are our own and we are answerable for them, are not to be measured by the distance a voice will carry or the fragile things our strength will crush. We have lived and we die; but we live on in the memory of men, a memory which may treasure a lie of ours that will endure for centuries doing its deadly work, a lie that must ultimately be damned to make way for truth. Our children live after us, and theirs after them. Who can say when the surge of our life dies out of theirs? The apostles preached for a few years before being crushed by the power of Rome; has the effect of that preaching yet stopped? The great heresiarchs—Arius, Luther, and the rest—were stopped by the barrier of death; their words and works were limited by the finite limits of a man's power, but the effects, which were their very own, are still being reaped by other harvesters though centuries have passed.

Something the same is true of the angels and the devils, for they play their part in the world of men and the actions of men. They have their work, a work of hate or of joy; they will have their rewards and punishments, meted out fully only when the last trace of that work has ceased to agitate or ennoble the world. The whole of a man's life is to be rewarded or punished, all of it; and the reward or punishment is given to the whole man, all of him, body and soul.

It is only when bodies and souls are reunited that the conquest of death has reached completion; only then can the last word be said on this conquest. It may seem odd that the word "conquest" has been insisted on again and again in this chapter. Really, no other word will do. It is a fighting word to describe a grand fight. Even in the physical sense, these two, life and death, are at each other's throat from the first instant of infant life; death is a threat, an enemy encroaching, an enemy who never gives up the fight. In the spiritual sense, the same battle of life and death, of virtue and sin, is on from the first dawn of reason; it is a struggle where no quarter is possible, no end in sight, until one or the other has lost.

It is not the kind of fight a man can stand aside and watch. There is no possibility of neutrality. He is plunged into it by his very manhood. He must take sides. It is paradoxical, but strictly true, that those who think too much of life, fight desperately on the side of death; those who think too much of the joy of life, fight unceasingly on the side of misery; those who think too much of the glimpse of heaven possible in this life, fight strongly for hell. Men must take sides and they do. Life or death must win in the career of every man. We have seen the results of the victory of life; how about the victory of death?

In the denial of the resurrection, that is, in the surrender of the palm of victory to death, there is a double note paralleling, at least on the surface, that of life's victory. There is, first of all, a note of relief, a sense of escape; one has succeeded in throwing off the stifling blanket of responsibility, escaped from the haunting possibility of evil into a world without barriers, a world of new freedom. Man no longer has to answer eternally for his life and his acts; he is free. But the note is false. It is a release that sets man at the mercy of his desire, delivers him up to the animal world, makes him the victim of a civil war within himself and of slavery from without.

Along with this sense of relief, there is a hopeless sadness, a penetrating, tragic thing patient of no consolation; for man is convinced that life, love, knowledge, accomplishment, justice, companionship and all the rest do have an end. Man cannot stand that sort of tragedy very long. He copes with it, in some cases, by unreasoning resignation which produces a fatalistic calm and creates its own ends of vague generalities to minister the small comfort of empty dreams. In other cases, he meets it with an eager, desperate draining of the cup of life before it be dashed from his hand. Or, finally, he arms himself with a cynical refusal to live a life which has no meaning; it is this attitude which takes its ghoulish satisfaction in a mocking disruption of the lives of others and the destruction of its own.

Both these notes of death's victory take the heart out of human living. The first, in the name of freedom, delivers a man to slavery, a fact easily verifiable in any "age of freedom." The second either squeezes the meat out of life, destroying man's taste for the very things he started out to clutch so eagerly—leisure, pleasure, power, and the rest; or, in the case of the fatalist, it makes life a ghostly thing, a hollow, haunted existence. In these victories of death, men must walk in the darkness of unreason, if they are to walk at all, or frankly face the despair of it and surrender unconditionally.

In a word, death has conquered life and made of it a grim masquerade of the living dead. The air, the odor, the very color of death in its corruption penetrate the deepest reaches of life; the blinding darkness of the tomb hovers over all; its doors are already closed forever.

In Christ, life has conquered death. The air, the odor, the very color of life enter into the darkest corner of the tomb. Death is a gateway, as is life; a motion to high goals, as is life; a fulfillment of hope, an unveiling of faith, a consummation of charity, as life never is. Life's promises are fulfilled by death's opening up of enduring life. The rehearsal is over, death lifts the curtain, and the eternal play is on.